PROFIT
FROM THE
CORE

PROFIT
FROM THE
CORE

Growth Strategy in
an Era of Turbulence

———

CHRIS ZOOK
with JAMES ALLEN

Harvard Business School Press

Boston, Massachusetts

Printed in the United States of America

04 03 02 01 00   5 4 3 2 1

Library of Congress Cataloging-in-Publication Data

Zook, Chris, 1951–

    Profit from the core : growth strategy in an era of turbulence /
Chris Zook with James Allen.

      p. cm.

    Includes bibliographical references and index.

    ISBN 1-57851-230-1 (alk. paper)

      1. Corporations—Growth. 2. Industrial management. 3. Corporate
profits. I. Allen, James, 1960– II. Title.

HD2746 .Z66 2001

658.15'5—dc21

                                           00-050584

The paper used in this publication meets the requirements of the
American National Standard for Permanence of Paper for Publications and Documents in Libraries and Archives Z39.48-1992.

Contents

Preface

When we embarked on a two-year project at Bain & Company to explore the key strategic decisions that most often determine growth or stagnation in business, we never intended to publish a book. But our clients, after hearing about the findings in presentations and management meetings, urged us to do so. Why? What did they see?

In part, these executives were responding to what they felt was a useful framework for understanding and addressing the key decision points encountered in growing a business. They thought this framework was practical and could be applied in their own companies to their own decisions. They especially valued the amount of empirical data backing up the conclusions, in high contrast to some of the more faddish, popular books that professed to offer the new elixir or silver bullet. More and more, these executives were finding that such "ideas de jour" were unproven, rushed to mass market before being tested, and, not surprisingly, generally ineffective at driving positive economic results in real businesses. Many of our clients were frustrated by the seemingly endless succession of distracting miracle cures and longed for a back-to-basics approach tailored to the contemporary business environment.

Encouraged by these reactions from people running businesses, we continued to develop our fact base on growth strategies to a point where it encompassed a ten-year database of more than eight thousand companies' growth histories, more than one hundred senior executives' conversations, and more than two hundred case studies conducted at Bain, Bain Capital, and elsewhere. And we further refined the framework in more client settings, in a series of Growth Breakfasts held in London, and in numerous management conferences.

In the course of conducting these case studies, we were particularly struck by the experiences of private equity firms like Bain Capital and Texas Pacific Group. These investment firms were obtaining extremely high economic returns by more than leverage and deal structure alone. Their best deals were in acquiring companies owned by parents who had given up on their growth prospects or who were unable to see the businesses in new ways, bottling up potential profitable growth. Partway through the project, Jimmy Allen took the position of CEO at eVolution Global Partners, an investment venture set up by Bain, Texas Pacific Group, and the preeminent venture capital firm Kleiner Perkins Caufield & Byers to help large companies realize growth opportunities locked in and around their core businesses. These private equity experiences reinforce our messages about growth and are the source of some examples in the book.

The more deeply we probed into why some companies grow profitably while others do not (sometimes in the presence of superior ingredients, on the surface), the more surprised we were by some of the conclusions we were reaching. And it was this, too, that clients were reacting to. Here are some examples.

We found that the odds of achieving sustained, profitable growth were much lower than we had believed and that most companies that are growing profitably today have relatively low odds, on average, of doing so over the next five or ten years. Most bursts of growth are ephemeral, and the most publicized cases of growth and value creation that we are bombarded with by the business press represent a small fraction of the population of companies. Yet all companies are struggling, in their own ways, with the problems of growth that we address in this book.

In addition, we found that the choice of the next hot industry was much less important in driving growth and profitability over the long term than were strategy, competitive position, reinvestment rates, and execution. Many of the most successful sustained growth companies are actually in lower growth businesses such as energy (Enron), basic services (ServiceMaster), beverages (Starbucks), clothing (The Gap), athletic gear (Nike), financial information (Reuters), pipelines (Williams Companies), engineering (Bechtel), food services (Aramark), and salty snacks (Frito-Lay). And under the surface, these companies were doing some of the most interesting and innovative things of all. Indeed, it might be precisely the difficulty of these market environments that elicits superior business creativity in the search for new growth out of their core businesses. We draw heavily on the growth strategies of these types of companies in this book.

Some of the results were quite counterintuitive to us. For instance, narrower focus and concentration of resources on a single core business, rather than proliferation of investments in hot markets, proved the most frequent road to sustained, profitable growth. Focus to grow? And many of the strongest core businesses were the most prone to underperforming their full potential. The strongest are the most frequent underachievers?

Central to our findings are three ideas: the concept of a core business and its boundaries; the idea that every business has a level of full-potential performance that usually exceeds what the company imagines; and the idea that performance-yield loss occurs at many levels, from strategy to leadership to organizational capabilities to execution. We have focused strongly on the types of strategic business decisions that most often seem to tilt the odds of future success or disappointment.

Who Should Read This Book?

Executives running businesses where growth is an issue should read this book. We would hope that management teams can use the book, its data, its diagnostics, and its principles prior to engaging in strategy discussions to make more informed key decisions around the core issues of growth: (1) Where should we look for the next wave of profitable growth opportunities, and where might that lead? (2) How should we select from several different opportunities before us today? (3) What defines our business boundaries, and what is the measure of leadership that we strive to attain? (4) Is it time to consider redefining fundamentally some of the elements of our core business, and how should we go about doing that?

In addition, investors and analysts should find the frameworks and analogies useful in evaluating their own portfolios and asking the right questions.

Our Promise to Readers

An annual survey of decision tools and analytical techniques is conducted by our Bain colleague Darrell Rigby. Rigby has found that in any given year, about two hundred commonly applied business tools and frameworks are in use. That is no surprise. What is surprising, however, is the short life span of many of these tools that arise through a popular book or management fad, only to fail to be the magic elixir, constantly disappointing their Ponce de Leóns in search of the fountain of eternal business life. Moreover, these elixirs frequently have limited empirical support (they are new, so how can they?) and therefore rest only on a few reports of sightings of miracle cures.

Our promise is that we will not offer yet another such false hope. What we do offer is a collection of growth strategy ideas that presents a call back to the basics. We believe that the content of this book reveals the most common growth strategy errors and can help companies both improve their odds of success and reduce their odds of catastrophic failure. Our focus is on achieving results and reliability through making good strategic decisions. We believe that business awards few points for artistic merit.

The same choice of proven principles versus new ideas is true in most areas of human endeavor. Take golf, for instance. We believe that the typical golfer will benefit the most from a thorough grounding in Ben Hogan's "Five Elements of a Good Golf Swing," possibly with some modern computer-aided diagnostics set against those same time-proven principles. Mastering the basics and avoiding fatal flaws is less fun but more productive, we believe, than buying the most exotic composite-shaft club guaranteed to hit farther and straighter from any lie of the ball.

The same is true in business: there exist lasting principles and ideas that can drive profit from the core.

Expanding from the Core

Above all else, our ultimate goal is to provide a set of practical, tested, and reliable tools and ideas for executives to use in evaluating or redesigning their growth strategies. Some of these tools are contained in the book. However, there are others, such as software for organizing and displaying strategic growth options, that are more difficult to deliver in the form of a printed page. Consequently, we invite you to visit our Web site, <**www.profitfromthecore.com**>, where we provide additional materials and examples as well as an interactive tool to help you organize and display growth strategy options that you might be considering in your own business. At this site, you will also be able to link directly to the authors for follow-up. Best of luck to all in the pursuit of sustained, profitable growth.

Acknowledgments

Our first debt of gratitude is to the clients of Bain & Company who allow us to participate on a daily basis with them on the front lines of some of the most dynamic and challenging business battlegrounds. It is to these smart and hardworking executives, some in seemingly impossible jobs, that we dedicate this book.

We also thank our partners at Bain & Company. Although we did the writing of the book on our own time, the data, client contacts, anecdotes, and support infrastructure are all Bain. Our first version of this acknowledgment, which included the name of each person who contributed an anecdote, advice, or idea, listed more than eighty individuals. So we abandoned the idea of the itemized list, opting instead for this single heartfelt and deep thank you.

We especially are grateful to Tom Tierney, former managing director at Bain, who encouraged our writing of this book from the beginning. Steve Schaubert, our mentor and a senior Bain director, was one of the first to suggest this project and has been our most constant muse. Steve read every draft, generously leaving thoughtful and extensive voice-mail messages the next day in response. Darrell Rigby has been a copilot through the entire project. He urged us to consider writing a book. Darrell has contributed ideas, material, contacts, wisdom, and friendship throughout.

Bain Capital, and especially Mitt Romney and Steve Pagliuca, were generous in sharing their experiences and making available to us case studies from their investment experiences.

Marci Taylor is the researcher who worked directly with Chris on the Bain Growth Project and continued to provide support through the full duration of the book's gestation period. She has added insight, accuracy, and inspiration whenever needed.

In addition, we have been blessed with excellent research assistants for support on specific pieces of work throughout. Tanya Lipiainen assembled and managed the database of eighty-four hundred companies. She also responded patiently whenever we requested "one more analysis." Murthy Nukala and Aditya Joshi were the first research associates to help with some of the original analyses that spurred this project forward.

Brenda Davis typed much of the manuscript, made editorial suggestions, provided psychological counseling, and has been the perfect assistant in every way. Katie Smith-Milway is the wonderful editor at Bain who assisted Chris with refining the second draft of the manuscript and who advised us throughout.

Our editors at the Harvard Business School Press, Melinda Adams Merino, Barbara Roth, Sylvia Weedman, and Marjorie Williams, have provided inspiration when it mattered and have patiently nursed us through our first attempt to write a book. Thank you. In addition, we thank Walter Kiechel for urging us to write a book on growth several years ago, when he first saw our early Bain presentation.

We especially wish to thank Donna, Chris's wife, who allowed her dining room table to become "ground zero" for the most intense writing phase, which also displaced our wonderful families in some way on a regular basis.

Finally, Chris thanks his father, Nicholas Zook, a newspaperman and writer, for patiently trying to teach his son to write—perhaps the toughest task of all.

1

Desperately Seeking Growth

Have you managed to grow your business profitably during the recent boom but find yourself running out of obvious paths to more and more profitable growth? Or do you feel pressured to initiate business activity in the Internet economy but find yourself worried about choosing the right activity to target while also minimizing distraction from your core business? Perhaps you feel that your core business has untapped profit growth potential, but you are not sure how to determine where it is. Or perhaps your industry is changing in a way that makes you wonder whether it might soon be time to redefine the business model that has been so productive for so many years. But then the question is, how can you manage a path of profitable growth through the transition?

If you can see your company in any of these situations, the findings of this book may surprise and interest you. The most important issue faced by all management teams is how to grow their companies. As we enter the twenty-first century, the odds against winning the growth game are worse than ever, in spite of the unprecedented success of the economy. Consider how the goal posts have moved for management:

- The value shareholders now assign to companies, which represents an average of twenty-six times their earnings, demands that those companies grow at a rate three to four times that of the GDP.

- Investors are giving management teams less time than ever to prove themselves. For instance, shareholders are shifting in and out of stocks at five times the rate they did a few decades ago (every six days in the case of Internet economy stocks), demanding not merely growth but growth each and every quarter.

- Even in the best of times, our analysis shows that nine of ten management teams fail to grow their companies profitably. Given investor expectations of quarter-by-quarter growth, ninety-nine of one hundred management teams will fail to meet shareholder expectations.

Ironically, the space between the goal posts is narrowing and shifting, and this is happening just as management is experiencing unprecedented difficulties putting players on the field and keeping them there:

- Management has been hit with defections of the best talent and finds it increasingly difficult to attract and retain new employees. The average tenure for someone in information technology, the "star player" in the Internet economy, is now only thirteen months.

- Even the coaches—the CEOs themselves—are remaining in a given job for only one-third the time they did as recently as a decade ago.

Finally, the rules of the game are continually changing. As we demonstrate later in this book, turbulence in industries has increased by a factor of four.

It is no wonder, then, that participants in a game that's impossible to play, much less win, are now particularly receptive to the soothing, dulcimer tones of pundits who suggest deceptively simple (and consistently incorrect) strategies for winning an extremely complex, multifaceted game. Their siren song seduces with its revolutionary appeal: "discard the old, leave your historic core business behind and set out for the promised land." Sometimes this advice leads to the right course. Yet, as we argue in this book and demonstrate with examples and extensive empirical data, it usually *does not* solve the fundamental problem and can even aggravate the underlying cause of inadequate profitable growth. Like the ancient mariners of the *Odyssey,* those managers who respond to the siren song of growth can experience brief periods of euphoria. But when they finally awaken to reality, they often find themselves heading straight for the shoals.

We have found that the key to unlocking hidden sources of growth and profits is not to abandon the core business but to focus on it with renewed vigor and a new level of creativity. We have also found that often the most successful businesses are at greatest risk of succumbing to the siren song. Consider the following examples of four companies that have moved away from a core business in search of greener pastures.

Case 1: Bausch & Lomb

Bausch & Lomb got started in the ophthalmic business in 1853, when German immigrant Jacob Bausch opened a small store in Rochester, New York, to sell European optical imports. Over the next 120 years, the business developed slowly and carefully, step by step, just like the work of the meticulous eye doctors that it served. By 1973, Bausch & Lomb had grown to $235 million in sales and was the leader in its instrument and lens businesses.

Then everything changed. In the mid-1970s, Bausch & Lomb obtained from an independent Czechoslovakian scientist the patents for *spin casting,* a process for making soft contact lenses. Spin casting not only produced lenses that were more comfortable than those on the market but did so at a lower cost. At the time, the standard procedure for creating a lens was to lathe it from a button of hard plastic. With spin casting, a drop of polymer is spun in a shaped dish and then stabilized under ultraviolet light to make the lens. The lenses created are "soft" because the liquid polymer sets in a form that is softer and more flexible than that of the hard plastic used in lathing. These more flexible lenses have proven to be better for the health of the eye and are easier for the optometrist to fit. They have also allowed for greater productivity throughout the value chain, from manufacturer to end user.

The soft contact lens was one of those breakthroughs that crack open and transform the competitive dynamics and market size in an industry. Throughout the mid-1980s, Bausch & Lomb developed and executed brilliant strategy, driving one competitor after another out of the market and causing others, locked into high-cost lathing methods, to disinvest in the business. The company's share of new lens fittings rose to 40 percent of the market, several times larger than that of its nearest competitors, American Hydron and Coopervision. Bausch & Lomb continued to invest in the business, buying the leading manufacturer of gas-permeable lenses, Polymer Technologies, to round out its product line. The company became a darling of Wall Street, outperforming the market over this period by more than 200 percent, with high, growing, and consistent earnings reports.

Then, as competitors began attacking its position with new technologies such as cast molding (also a low-cost method), Bausch & Lomb began to divert its attention from its core business, spending the cash flow from its lens and solutions businesses in new areas. "The core business is eroding, margins will erode as competitors enter. . . . Use the cash to find new sources of growth," sang the sirens. The management team invested in products sold by other health professionals, such as electric toothbrushes, skin ointments, and hearing aids, but they established no obvious linkage between these products and the core lens business.

Slowly but surely, with resources and management attention distracted, Bausch & Lomb's contact lens business flattened out. The stock that had risen from $3 per share in 1973 to $56 per share in 1991 plummeted to less than $33 per share. Moreover, Johnson & Johnson entered the contact lens business by heavily funding a new acquisition, Vistakon, with a new product idea: disposable lenses. Of course, disposable lenses are not much different from regular lenses except that they are sold at a lower price in packages of twelve or twenty-four. What better company to have introduced this product than the one-time cost and technology leader, Bausch & Lomb? Instead, Bausch & Lomb's market share declined to 16 percent, which put the company in third place behind Johnson & Johnson and Ciba Vision. At first, Bausch & Lomb reacted with desperate measures, slashing prices and turning to channel management. Then it changed its management team.

The new team has acted swiftly to solve the company's problems, exiting the noncore businesses, including hearing aids, dental devices, and sunglasses sold directly to consumers. The cover of its 1998 annual report redefined Bausch & Lomb's corporate mission, presenting the company as the "Eyes of the World." The catchphrase represents the company's return to its original core business, through which it hopes to reignite growth and regain market share. But precious ground, time, and capital have been lost. Even more important, new and strong competitors are now entrenched. And it probably did not have to be this way.

Case 2: Amazon.com

Amazon.com appears in the popular press almost daily, sometimes as the poster child of the Internet economy, sometimes as an example of the complex choices facing a young company with a new-to-the-world business model. The drama is still playing out, raising questions about whether the siren song of growth has Amazon under its spell.

The company got its start, as most everyone knows, with the online selling of a product with a notoriously inefficient, multitier distribution channel: books. The typical offline bookstore returns more than 40 percent of the books that appear on its shelves for credit. The reasons returns are so high are that it is impossible for bookstores to predict which titles will become bestsellers and that a large number of "standard" books must be stocked in inefficient lots of two or three. The Amazon model bypasses this inefficiency by centralizing distribution and by getting its money from the consumer up front, often before the publisher needs to be paid. Moreover, Jeff Bezos, Amazon's CEO, recognized that Amazon had the potential to be more than just a low-cost channel for book purchasing. With the introduction of book reviews written by customers, Amazon made itself a community Web site through which consumers could voice their views about the books they were purchasing. Based on the power of this business model, market capitalization rose to more than $30 billion in 1999 on $500 million of sales. During this period, Amazon increased the stakes, trying to become what Bezos calls "a place where you can buy anything and everything."

Suddenly, Amazon no longer confined itself to targeting the inefficient, multistep value chain of the bookseller (and, somewhat later, the video store); it began to compete with Wal-Mart and The Home Depot. Amazon moved with lightning speed into power tools, consumer electronics, garden furniture, and even cosmetics. A Bain analysis based on a survey of 1,200 consumers has shown a positive cash payback period of under two years for acquisition of book buyers online, as well as a palpable economic competitive advantage and increasing customer loyalty based on Amazon's services and its personalization software. Thus far, however, the loyalty model in these new product lines remains unproved. Will Amazon's new "all things to all people" model pay off? Or, as we suggest in this book, should Amazon have been faithful to its roots and focused on expanding its core business? Time will tell. In the meantime, cumulative losses have mounted to $1.2 billion, and investor nervousness is high, reflected in a 70 percent stock price decline.

Case 3: Cooke Optics

Cooke Optics was founded in England in 1890 for the purpose of creating the highest-quality lenses for still photography, a new and fast-growing market at the time. Cooke quickly became the gold standard in the industry, and the camera taken to the South Pole in 1907 by explorer Sir Ernest Shackleton and his crew was fitted with a Cooke lens. During World War I, Cooke lenses were critical for high-resolution aerial photography. The advent of silent films put Cooke lenses on the front of many cameras in leading movie studios. As the small company evolved, it expanded into specialized zoom lenses and even higher-quality "prime" nonzoom lenses. In 1946, Cooke was sold to the Rank Group, a company with no related holdings or interest in preserving Cooke's quality image. Over the next few decades, Rank moved into postproduction studios, resorts, and casinos, leaving Cooke at the end of the line when it came to getting attention from management or resources for investment. Cooke stagnated. Comparing this state of affairs with the company's proud history, a thirty-seven-year employee lamented, "The place was so run down that sea-gull feathers would float down through the holes in the roof."[1] The company was finally rescued in 1998 by Les Zellan, a theater-lighting specialist who had kept an eye on Cooke for decades, watching its once-valuable core business erode. In 1998, he got his chance and took it, buying Cooke for only $3 million. Since then, the core lens business, neglected for nearly five decades, has been brought back to life with a new lens that has superior focusing technology. The lens caught on almost immediately and has been used for shooting such recent hit films as *Angela's Ashes, The Cider House Rules, The Hurricane,* and *Erin Brockovich.*

Case 4: The Gartner Group

The Gartner Group was founded in 1979 by Gideon Gartner, a stock analyst at the securities trading firm of Oppenheimer who specialized in tracking IBM and its few competitors in those days. The original purpose of the Gartner Group was to sell information on IBM to investment bankers and stock brokers. Shortly after the founding of the company, its focus was broadened to include customers deciding on equipment to buy or starting negotiations with IBM for hardware. In the burgeoning market for business computers, consumer need proved to be large, and Gartner focused entirely on becoming, in a sense, a consumer clearinghouse for customer data and expert opinion on products.

Saatchi & Saatchi purchased the company in the mid-1980s as part of its attempt to unify consulting and advertising services in a single company—a misconceived growth strategy in itself that soon imploded. Saatchi became disillusioned with the consulting business in 1989 and sold Gartner to Bain Capital, a private equity firm specializing in buying noncore or undermanaged corporate assets.

For $60 million, Bain Capital purchased a company that was growing at about 15 percent annually, had reached $55 million in revenues, and had margins of only about 10 percent, a disappointment to its former parent. But Bain Capital saw something more in the Gartner Group than a small, low-margin consultancy. The more Bain managers studied the company's core business, the more they began to believe that Gartner would have a much greater opportunity for growth and for margin expansion if they looked at it not as a consulting business but as a vehicle for collecting, packaging, and distributing high-value syndicated data.

Under the ownership of Bain Capital, Gartner refocused on becoming a consumer clearinghouse for customer responses and an honest broker of advice on hardware and software purchases. Gartner's growing company subscriber base gave it proprietary access to thousands of companies whose managers were willing to comment for the record on their experiences with buying and installing computer systems. No longer did a corporate management information system department need to commission expensive outside consulting studies for the purpose of obtaining objective data; it could rely on Gartner studies, which were less costly and more timely than its own. Gartner built strong barriers to imitation through its subscriber base and its database of benchmarks that allowed it to expand its margins from about 10 percent to 30 percent.

Bain had a three-part growth strategy for Gartner:

1. Turn Gartner into a syndicated data and research company with a much more scalable model than consulting

2. Expand geographically beyond its high East Coast customer concentration into the West and Europe by adding salespeople

3. Deepen the product line in the most leveraged, vertical, industry-focused application markets

The suggested strategy of looking at the original core business in a new way was successful. The company grew from $55 million in 1980 to $295 million in 1995 under Bain's ownership to $734 million in 1999 as a public company. Over this period, Gartner solidified its hold in its core business. Bain Capital sold the company to Dun & Bradstreet for approximately a twenty times return on its equity, and Dun & Bradstreet subsequently sold Gartner in an initial public offering at an additional twenty times multiple.

What is notable about this growth story, other than the four hundred times return on equity invested, is the fact that the new owners had a different take on the core business, seeing it as a syndicated data and research enterprise rather than a consultancy. The ability to creatively see the core in a new light and act on it is a theme that we will return to throughout this book.

Our Mission

In each of the above cases, and hundreds of others that we have examined, we see a tendency for strong core businesses to lose momentum by virtue of premature abandonment, miscalculation, or overreaching in search of new growth. Our intention in this book is not to suggest that we have a one-size-fits-all solution for problems with growth. Rather, our intention is to suggest that many of the common cures prescribed in the popular business literature need to be balanced against the weight of evidence on real company experiences. What we offer is a set of practical and proven principles, diagnostic tests, and questions for management teams to use as tools for reexamining or revising their strategies in search of the next wave of profitable growth. In our quest to understand the dynamics of growth, we drew on the following fact base:

- About two hundred case studies in Bain & Company and in the public record

- Interviews and discussions with about one hundred senior executives

- A database of 1,854 public companies in seven countries followed over ten years

- Numerous pieces of focused empirical analysis concerning sources of profitable growth

- The records of many private equity firms, including Bain Capital, which generously shared many of its case studies with us

- Extensive examination of the existing literature (cited throughout the book) and of secondary data

The lack of empirical data behind many business "cure-alls" has prompted one Oxford don to proclaim management science a "phony academic subject, a shallow contemporary shibboleth promoting a noxious cant."[2] We are not that cynical. We consider management science to be highly productive, but we also understand that it is in its infancy. More important, we maintain that there do exist a few lasting principles of business strategy that have clearly driven results year after year, that apply across a wide range of industries, and that explain the results of both success and failure. Some of these principles need to be adapted for the purposes of the Internet economy, but in most cases, the fundamental underpinnings of microeconomics endure.

Defining Profitable Growth

We explored many definitions of profitable growth and settled on one that involves several dimensions. Throughout this book, we define *sustained growth* as growth in both revenues and profits over an extended period of time while total shareholder returns (share price and dividend reinvestment) exceed the cost of capital. Empirically, few companies in the long term create shareholder value without earning their cost of capital.

When we looked at the data, we identified targets that were at or below most of the strategic planning targets we found in a survey of strategic plans. These targets are (1) achieving 5.5 percent real (inflation adjusted) growth in revenues and earnings and (2) earning one's cost of capital over an average of ten years. We examined the data company by company to control for accounting anomalies and one-time charges. The results of our screen are depicted in figure 1-1, showing the percentages of our full sample of companies that meet our revenue criterion, income criterion, and shareholder value creation criterion. Even with these relatively conservative and modest targets, we found that only about one company in eight, or 13 percent, achieved sustained and profitable growth (or could be classified as a sustained value creator) over a decade that many would rank as among the best for the world economy. In contrast, our internal sample of targets from strategic plans showed that more than 90 percent of the companies examined had aimed at returns well in excess of these levels.

When we tightened the criteria a bit more, requiring 8 percent real growth (about 11 percent to 12 percent nominal currency growth in most of our major countries in this period), the percentage of sustained value creators declined to only 9 percent. In a survey of strategic plans, we found that the target of more than two-thirds of the businesses examined was at least at these levels. Yet the reality is that fewer than one in ten achieved it.

We found that companies that grew revenues but not profits did not create economic value in the long term (though they can create

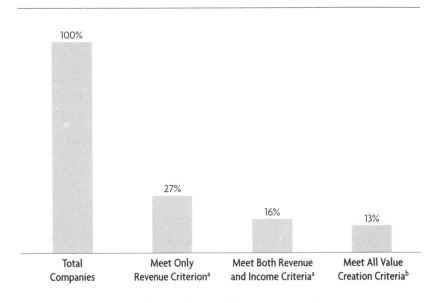

1-1 Few Companies Achieve Sustainable Growth Strategies

Source: Worldscope database, Bain analysis.

Note: Database includes companies with > $500 million in revenues in seven countries (United States, Australia, United Kingdom, France, Germany, Italy, and Japan) for which a full set of data is available.
[a] Compound annual growth rate > 5.5 percent, 1988–1998.
[b] Average annual total shareholder return (stock price appreciation + dividends paid on $1 invested) − cost of capital > 0, 1988–1998.

shareholder wealth in the short term in the stock market). Companies that grew profits but not revenues were on an unsustainable growth path that eventually petered out. Companies that grew both revenues and profits but did not earn their cost of capital eventually (recall that our period of analysis is ten years) lost their ability to find investors.[3] An extensive body of work on investor value creation supports this point of view.

Other measures of profitable growth that we considered are worth noting, along with their specific limitations. Stock price growth (adjusted for splits) is alluringly simple, but it can be manipulated by share buyback that neither affects the total enterprise value nor creates growth. Total enterprise market value growth is somewhat better. However, it is possible to grow total market value through mergers that neither help earnings nor create a sustained growth trajectory. Moreover, putting together several poorly performing companies to create a new one is not what our project was about.

Share of total industry profits or share of total industry value is an interesting measure of relative competitive success. However, it does not take into account absolute levels of growth or profitability, which could be declining. Moreover, it begs the question of the business boundaries, of what to include or exclude.

High total shareholder return is critical to sustained, profitable growth. Yet a company that did not grow, had no assets, and had positive cash flow would have infinite returns. Looking at returns in the absence of growth is as limiting in the context of our study as looking at growth in the absence of returns.

Finally, there are more specialized or exotic measures of profitable growth. One such measure is profit or value creation per employee. But this is at least as much a function of labor and capital intensity of the business as it is of sustained, profitable growth. A derivative measure of this is growth in value per employee. This, however, could be as much a function of shifting to more capital intensity as it is of performance and growth. These are interesting measures, but not what we were after.

Using the screen of earning the cost of capital in the long term and growing both revenues and profits worked well for us, though we urge management teams to supplement this metric with others, both short term and long term, in considering their own growth pattern.

Defining the Core

It is our thesis in this book that the foundation of sustained, profitable growth is a clear definition of a company's core business. A business can be defined from two related perspectives. The first (outside-in) is from the point of view of the outside world, with natural business boundaries defined by underlying market economics. The second (inside-out) is from the point of view of those inside the company, with the company's business boundaries defined by its unique core.

Here is an example of the distinction. Enterprise Rent-A-Car, Alamo Rent a Car, and Avis are clearly in a business that external criteria define as car rental. The business involves purchasing and managing fleets, running automated reservation centers, managing a branch network, and serving customers who rent cars for various purposes. Within this business, however, the three companies have different cores. Enterprise has a 70 percent share of the market for insurance replacement and repair rentals. The company got its start in this distinct segment, building its suburban locations and business model to meet the needs of body shops and insurance companies. Alamo's core business comes from leisure renters, who don't mind having to pick up their rental cars at locations other than airports. The company situates its branches in popular vacation destinations such as Orlando, Florida. Avis's core is airport rentals. It sells heavily to corporate renters requiring speedy service, newer cars, a variety of business amenities, and, obviously, a network of prime airport locations. Each of these companies would view its core differently, and each would be right. Yet each participates in a rental car business that external economics is treating more and more as one competitive arena.

A different type of example is Gillette, which has had men's shaving products as its core business since its founding nearly one hundred years ago. After achieving a 70 percent market share in its core, Gillette sought growth in an unconventional way, looking beyond the limited shaving market. It redefined its core business more in terms of control and share of the checkout counter displays at retail stores, leading it to expand into writing instruments, Duracell batteries, and other distribution-related products. The jury is out on the full success of this strategy. However, it is a case in which a company has redefined its core such that it no longer sits within the external boundaries marked on the map held by the rest of the business world.

To identify your core business, first identify the five following assets:

1. Your most potentially profitable, franchise customers

2. Your most differentiated and strategic capabilities

3. Your most critical product offerings

4. Your most important channels

5. Any other critical strategic assets that contribute to the above (such as patents, brand name, position at a control point in a network)

When we begin a consulting assignment at Bain, we almost always ask first: "What is the business definition where you compete?" "What is your core business and source of potential competitive advantage?" The answers to these questions require an understanding of each of the five dimensions.

A recent *Wall Street Journal* article announced "Corporate America Confronts the Meaning of a 'Core' Business." The article goes on to recognize the complexity inherent in this task, noting: "Focus is in these days, both on Wall Street and in boardrooms across America, and this raises a surprisingly complex question: What constitutes a core business? Is it a product? A cache of intellectual property? A process? Or, is it a business design . . . that can be deployed across multiple industries?"[4]

For some companies, definition of the core business is not overly difficult; for others, it is extremely vexing. For all, it is important to have the clearest definition possible. In the case of Gillette, the core business would appear to be men's shaving products. This part of Gillette's business was its fastest growing and most profitable component in 1910, and it remains so today. The key assets that constitute this core include some deep areas of competence such as expertise in the manufacturing of high-precision miniature items, proficiency in blade sharpening and handling technology, and skill in brand management. Gillette has used these assets to enter a variety of related businesses ranging from hair care products (Toni) to small electronic appliances (Braun) to toothbrushes (Oral-B) to batteries (Duracell). In some cases, as we discuss later in the book, these expansions were successful and drew on Gillette's core strength; in others, they proved unrelated distractions.

Companies such as Coca-Cola, Black & Decker, Ford, Vodafone, Dell Computer, Boeing, Starbucks, Wal-Mart, and even Bain & Company have relatively well-defined cores that most executives can understand and use as platforms for profitable growth. In some companies, such as PepsiCo, there may be several different and distinct cores—in this case, the cola business and the salty snacks business of Frito-Lay.

For other companies such as AOL Time Warner, 3M, Vivendi, Universal, General Electric, and Tyco, however, the core business is much more difficult to define. These companies are the exception. Moreover, these types of highly complex or conglomeratelike companies are seldom found in the ranks of sustained value creators. General Electric, under the direction of Jack Welch, is a clear exception—a company that has been able to sustain multiple cores, several of which would be large scale on their own, their glue being the management processes and people management systems that define GE.

Most conglomerates have not been able to manage multiple strong cores successfully. Conglomerates are underrepresented among our sustained value creators, consistent with the findings of many past studies on diversification. Moreover, we find that, overwhelmingly, the strongest performing companies have leading positions in one, or at most two, core businesses that they drive into adjacent territory step by step, simultaneously strengthening the original core as they extend it to new customers, channels, products, or applications.

For the purposes of this book, we define the *core business* as that set of products, capabilities, customers, channels, and geographies that defines the essence of what the company is or aspires to be to achieve its growth mission—that is to grow its revenue sustainably and profitably. We recognize that this is a loose definition that can lead to significant debate among management teams. There can be tension between what a company is and what it aspires to or needs to be for competitive reasons. And there is often a lack of proportion in the number of customers overall and the number of customers who really support profits—the classic 80/20 rule, which states that less than 20 percent of a customer base accounts for 80 percent of a company's profits. Inversely, this implies that most customers often do not define the core business; that is, they do not contribute to the growth mission. The essence of a company's growth strategy is to define the core business as we have defined it and to pour company resources into this core business until it achieves its full potential.

How to Approach This Book

In this book, we focus on a single theme: the extraordinary importance of creating a strong core business as a foundation for driving company growth.

We define the growth metrics that management should use precisely—the goal of management is to grow revenues and profits sustainably. Only this will create shareholder value over the long term. We define the core business as precisely as possible, emphasizing that the process of defining the core business is at the heart of what a management team must do and is inherently an imprecise science.

We fully acknowledge that the theme of seeking profit from the core is not new, and throughout the book we acknowledge extensive work done by others on this and related topics. We feel compelled to return to the theme for three reasons. First, the empirical data on the frequency with which management teams undervalue their core business is overwhelming. Why are their expectations so low? Second, focusing solely on a strong core business is necessary to but not sufficient for achieving sustainable growth. Management teams constantly meet with opportunities to move into related businesses, and at times such moves are absolutely necessary to strengthen the core and add new profit streams. How should management teams respond to this basic tension in business—when to focus on the core, when to pursue adjacent opportunities? Third, a management team must sometimes choose to make a fundamental change in the essence of the company's core business if it is to create new and sustainable growth. This is especially the case in any industry experiencing turbulent times. How should managers think about this decision—which involves more risk than any other they will make—to change the core in the interest of protecting the core?

To address these questions, we have structured this book around the three basic issues management must face in seeking profit from the core:

1. Build market power and influence in the core business or in a segment of that business.

2. Having done that, expand into logical and reinforcing adjacencies around the core.

3. Shift or redefine the core in response to industry turbulence.

In chapter 2, we discuss how to define a core business and illustrate how to obtain the full potential from a core business. We introduce the first paradox of growth: *The better performing of your business units are likely to be those operating the furthest below their full potential.* We have found that when most management teams seek to revitalize the growth of a company, they focus on the underperforming business units. We argue that growth requires focusing instead on increasing the performance of the best businesses, no matter how well they are doing at present. The best business is in the best position to deliver better growth.

We begin by presenting evidence that a strong core is the key source of competitive advantage and then go on to define core business boundaries, means for differentiation through gaining market power and influence, and reasons why many of the best core businesses often are performing below their full growth potential and have a set of classic sources of "hidden value." In turbulent industry situations, however, the ability to define the boundaries of a core business becomes more challenged and the importance of traditional measures of market share, therefore, less relevant. In many traditional industries, competition among identical business models is the rule, yet more and more today we are observing competition among fundamentally different business models. Dealing with this increased competitive complexity is one of the primary issues facing business strategists in many industries.

In chapter 3, we shift to the topic of what we call "adjacency expansion," moving into a set of new but related businesses around the core business. In discussing adjacency expansion, we introduce the second paradox of growth: *The stronger your core business, the more opportunities you have both to move into profitable adjacencies and to lose focus.* Chapter 3 examines the typical patterns exhibited by those companies with the best records of historical growth. Some businesses, such as ServiceMaster and Reuters, have grown for decades, if not longer, by systematically expanding into logical business adjacencies around a relatively stable core. We reinforce the findings of dozens of studies with our own data showing how many of the most promising growth strategies were derailed by overexpansion or choice of the wrong adjacency. Industry turbulence, however, sometimes makes it necessary for managers to place more bets at the periphery of the business to hedge against uncertainties instead of marching forward on a planned path for growth, year after year, as seen in the expansion of stores in retail.

In chapter 4, we address when and how to redefine a core business, especially when faced with industry turbulence. Here we introduce the third paradox of growth: *The management teams that have been most successful in building a strong core business and that have benefited from adjacency expansion are also the most vulnerable to industry turbulence.* In some ways, this theme of redefinition runs *sotto voce* throughout every chapter of the book. The record of long-lived strong core businesses successfully redefining themselves and reasserting leadership is not an encouraging one for legacy companies.

Chapter 4 also examines the increasingly close linkage between organization and growth strategy. In these situations of turbulence and short response times, the popular epithet "structure follows strategy" is being rewritten as "sometimes structure *determines* strategy." The ability to react quickly and refine strategy based on marketplace events is a major source of competitive advantage for many successful companies.

In chapter 5, we provide some guidelines for the process of developing and refining growth strategy. We also conclude with the fourth paradox of growth: *All organizations inhibit growth.* In today's turbulent business environment, change—in company strategies, structures, and people—is crucial to achieving sustained profitable growth. To master change, managers must pursue it, not resist it.

While the message of profit from the core is simple, the challenges management faces in translating it into action are extraordinary. Each paradox of growth threatens to defeat management, to decrease the odds of achieving sustainable, profitable growth. The failure rate is as high as 99 percent.

We believe that the three elements of growth strategy listed above are as relevant to stable industries, such as food processing or textiles, in a long-term equilibrium as they are to turbulent industries, ranging from electric utilities to online retail, careening from disequilibrium to disequilibrium. However, in turbulent conditions many of the common strategic rules of thumb need to be adapted.

A great deal of excellent work has been done by academic researchers and business practitioners on the topic of how traditional rules of strategy, first developed for a stable, capital-intensive industry, now must be adapted for businesses facing the need to redefine themselves (especially information-intense businesses) around economic turbulence. For instance, Clayton Christensen has described brilliantly how new competitors can emerge and thrive using "disruptive" technologies, building power in low-profit marginal customers as the incumbent helplessly watches on.[5] Carl Shapiro has described how the peculiar economics of information businesses require a new set of economic rules to develop robust business strategies.[6] Others have examined why large companies are slow to adapt to change or why market share is less important than it used to be. Throughout the book we gratefully acknowledge and build on this foundational work.

We have referred repeatedly to the paradoxical aspects of growth strategy in business. Certainly, the world is full of paradoxes. To hit a golf ball farther, you hold the club looser. To make a plane lift off, you pull back on the throttle. To right a car during an icy skid, you take your foot off the brake. To make a plant grow stronger and more quickly, you cut it back. To create the most organized economy in the world, you allow the free market to work its magic.

Overlying all of the analysis in this book is a final paradox: *From focus comes growth; by narrowing scope one creates expansion.* It is remarkable to us how, despite the array of growth opportunities presenting themselves to most management teams, the most reliable and consistent solution is to profit from the core.

2

The Profitable Core

The idea of a core set of economic activities is as old as management science itself. David Ricardo's writings in 1817 on comparative advantage in trade were, in part, an attempt to determine the core set of activities around which a nation should focus its resources. Alfred Marshall's work in the late 1800s on increasing returns to scale anticipates the idea of business definition and competitive advantage from a growing core. Economists in the 1930s and 1940s examining antitrust matters constantly encountered the issues of business definition and how far market power extended from a core business. During the 1980s, an era of breakup artists and corporate restructuring, many business writers, such as Michael Porter, documented how corporations' returns declined as their activities became more diffuse and their core became less well defined.

More recently the idea of focusing on the core has been emphasized in writings ranging from the stick-to-your-knitting theme of *In Search of Excellence* to the work on core competence by Hamel and Prahalad to the idea of a central core vision in *Built to Last*. The central finding of our work is the strength of the evidence showing how often profitable growth is fueled by a strong core—the stronger and more focused, the better. In the rest of this book we discuss how to define and strengthen a core, how to determine the best growth opportunities emanating out from a core, and when to step back and redefine the core.

The Power of Focusing on the Core

Companies that have very few, highly focused, core businesses account for most of the sustained growth companies. The historical record shows that most diversified companies should narrow and focus their activities to create fewer growth platforms, while companies with multiple mediocre business positions should restructure their portfolios to develop a single strong core. The evidence clearly supports this viewpoint.

- Most companies that sustain value creation possess only one or two strong cores.

- Private equity companies often achieve their greatest success by buying orphan businesses from diffuse conglomerates, thereby creating focus.

- Spin-offs usually create both focus and value.

- Diversification is associated with lower average valuations than are typical of companies with focused cores.

- The few companies that became smaller and still created value are those that restructured to focus on a strong core, often eventually to turbocharge their growth again.

Evidence from Sustained Value Creators

An examination of the companies that have sustained both value creation and at least 5.5 percent annual growth over ten years shows that nearly 80 percent of these sustained value creators had one core business with clear market leadership (figure 2-1). These businesses were the source of most of their companies' profitable growth. Another 17

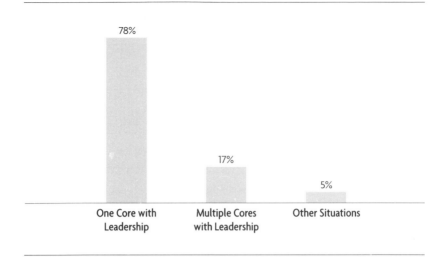

2-1 Sustained Value Creators Lead in Their Cores

Source: Worldscope database, OneSource, industry reports, Bain analysis.

Note: Core is defined as the business that creates a majority of the company's revenues. *Leadership* is defined as relative market share >1.2.

percent of sustained value creators had multiple cores around which they built their growth. Conglomerates, or highly diversified companies, appeared in only 5 percent of the sustained value creators, as compared to 21 percent in non–sustained value creators. The most notable example of a successful highly diverse company is General Electric, a collection of dominant core businesses. But General Electric is virtually unique among conglomerates for its performance in the past decade or century. In fact, it is the only company listed among the original Dow Jones industrials in the late 1800s that remains on the index. Moreover, most of its value creation in recent years was in one dominant business—GE Capital.

Many of the sustained value creators that we examined followed a common pattern: a tightly focused, sustained value creating company pulls farther and farther ahead of its rival, which is embedded in a diversified company with no clear focus or core. For example, in soft drinks, Pepsi (a food conglomerate until its recent breakup) trails Coke, a more focused competitor, in the soft drink business.

Anheuser-Busch leads in the beer business followed by Miller, which is part of a packaging foods conglomerate. Motorola and Ericsson, both companies with many separate parts, follow Nokia in the cellular phone business. Hewlett-Packard, a technology conglomerate until its recent spin-off, follows the maniacally focused Dell in personal computers. IBM and numerous other technology conglomerates follow EMC Corporation in data storage devices.

It is almost as if most growth strategies harbor a dark, destructive force that causes companies to reduce their focus on their core business and thereby to depart from the basis of their real differentiation. Consider the following questions: Why did Sears enter financial services while its once-dominant retail franchise was eroding? Why did GM purchase Electronic Data Systems when it was under the greatest pressure in its core automotive business? Why did Compaq Computer invest to buy Digital Equipment Corporation at a time when its core PC and server businesses were under the most severe attack from one of the toughest competitors on earth? These companies are run by smart people who must be familiar with the body of evidence proving the power of business focus and the need to outinvest competitors in their core business. So what happened?

Evidence from Private Equity

Impressive evidence of the strategic value of focusing on a strong core comes from companies that change their status from orphan businesses in large conglomerates to become freestanding businesses whose only cores are themselves. It is no wonder that private equity firms love to purchase noncore businesses from large conglomerates.

Consider the case of Accuride. Accuride sold truck rims and wheels to a concentrated number of original equipment manufacturer customers such as Ford, Volvo, General Motors, MAC, and Freightliner. Within Firestone Tire & Rubber Company, its previous owner, Accuride was an orphan. Its business was not even remotely related to any of Firestone's core tire or rubber businesses. Interestingly, it also competed against a number of other companies, such as

Goodyear and Budd, for which the steel rim-and-wheel business was also secondary. Did the noncore nature of these businesses provide a growth opportunity for a company that might choose to invest and manage Accuride differently? Bain Capital thought so.

Upon acquisition by Bain Capital, Accuride's focus changed. The company was cut loose from the budget constraints, management neglect, and low status it had experienced at Firestone. As Mitt Romney, managing director of Bain Capital, observes, "It was now a case of grow or perish."[1] Accuride's executives studied the market and economics in a new way. They concluded that if they could get close to 100 percent market share of several major customers, they could tilt industry dynamics in their favor and capture the majority of the industry's pool of profits for the long term. This, in turn, could discourage Goodyear and Budd from investing heavily in what was by no means their core business. And, of course, competitor disinvestment is a desirable outcome for any strategy.

To achieve their goals, the Accuride executives added low-cost capacity and preemptively offered lower prices and superior terms that competitors could not quickly match. Romney continues, "Goodyear acted slowly and decided not to match. Masco was stunned and stopped investing in plant capacity. I can remember a winter day walking around its deserted, partially completed site with snow-covered equipment. Budd did open a Mexican facility. But by then it was over—game, set and match."

Nowhere is the value of focus as clear as in a single-product company fighting for its life against less-focused competitors embedded in large conglomerates with many cross-cutting agendas and trade-offs. Accuride saw its market share relative to competitors go through the roof, its absolute share double, and its profitability rise 66 percent in fewer than two years. Bain Capital, for its insight into an undermanaged core business competing against other undermanaged core businesses, earned nearly twenty-five times return on its investment.

The power of focusing on the core proved a decisive factor in this success story. While there are few controlled experiments in business, because of the number of economics factors at play, there are many cases such as Accuride that demonstrate the power of reestablishing intense focus on a single core, building strength by acquiring competitors or by driving the profitable core through increased investment and a more aggressive strategy. Many of the most successful investments in the annals of leveraged buyouts and private equity firms stem from strategically undermanaged, noncore businesses (with profitable cores at their centers) that are purchased and revived by a new owner.

Evidence from Spin-offs

The experiences of companies that have split themselves up or spun off major divisions or groups as separate public companies offer still more evidence of the power of focus. David Sadtler, Andrew Campbell, and Richard Koch's examination of the aftermath of spin-offs found that they have led to an average 15 percent increase in the companies' relative competitive performance in the stock market.[2] In another study of more than one hundred companies that had undergone spin-offs, New York analyst Steven Bregman found that the spin-offs generated an annual rate of return from 1991 through 1996 of 37.2 percent, as compared to only a 17.5 percent increase in the Standard & Poor's index over the same period.[3]

PepsiCo provides an example of this positive spin-off effect. Over the past two decades, Coke has outperformed Pepsi substantially, even though Pepsi has performed well and provided total return to shareholders of 23 percent. Moreover, Pepsi's fast-food restaurant business was lagging in its performance and falling behind that of another focused competitor, McDonald's. In 1997, Pepsi spun off its $14 billion restaurant business, which consisted of Taco Bell, Kentucky Fried Chicken, and Pizza Hut.

Many who followed the company argued that the restaurant business was a drag on the beverage business and that the beverage businesses caused lack of focus on the noncore restaurants. One *Wall Street Journal* article even asserted that there was economic value destruction from the combination:

Some analysts argue that Pepsi is a distant second to Coke in the profitable fountain business—selling syrup to restaurants for their soda fountains—precisely because of its ownership of fast-food chains. Coke's sales force can tell a restaurant that by offering Pepsi-Cola drinks it is putting money in the pockets of competitors Taco Bell and Pizza Hut.[4]

Management acknowledged to the investors that the restaurant business was diverting too much attention and time from its need to focus on the core. CEO Roger Enrico admitted that "a whole lot more focus would be very beneficial."[5]

At the time, one article called the restaurant business "an anchor pulling through the sand at the bottom of the ocean."[6] But since the spin-off, both the original core and the new restaurant business, Tricon Global Restaurants, have done well, the latter outperforming its reference group of restaurants by a factor of two.

Evidence from Diversification Studies

Further evidence of the power of a strong, singular core comes from studies of the impact of shareholder value on diversification (the opposite of focus on the core). Probably the most thorough empirical study done was by Constantinos Markides, who examined the extent and effects of corporate refocusing in the 1980s. Defining *refocusing* as a company's deciding to reduce the scope of its activities in order to concentrate on the "core" business (that is, to reduce diversification), Markides found that more companies were refocusing in the 1980s than had done so in the 1960s. In the 1960s, only 1 percent of the top American companies were refocusing, while 25 percent were diversifying. In the 1980s, more than 20 percent of these companies were refocusing, while 8 percent were diversifying. In addition, his research showed that companies refocused by divesting unrelated businesses and acquiring related ones. Among the top one hundred U.S. companies from 1981 through 1987, more than

65 percent of acquisitions were related to the core business and nearly 58 percent of divestitures were unrelated to the core business. Markides also found that reducing diversification created market value, showing that a company's market value goes up nearly 2 percent on the day it announces it's refocusing.[7]

Michael Porter, in a study published in the *Harvard Business Review* in 1987, also looked at the contribution of diversification to corporate performance. Analyzing the diversification histories of thirty-three large U.S. companies from 1950 through 1986, he found dismal track records. In fact, these corporations, on average, had divested more than half of their acquisitions in new industries and more than 60 percent of their acquisitions in entirely new fields. The average divestment rate in unrelated acquisitions was even higher— nearly 75 percent.[8]

Evidence from Shrinking Value Creators

Our final validation of the power of focusing on the profitable core comes from analysis of the rare and transient group of shrinking value creators. These are the few companies (only 3 percent to 4 percent of our sustained value creators) whose real revenues shrank during the decade of our analysis but whose rates of value creation remained positive. Eighty-five percent of the shrinking value creators in our database followed the same formula: they shrank their company down to a subset of businesses clustered around an original core. One example is Sears, which decided to divest its financial services businesses as it was working to revive its core retail business. Another is General Dynamics, which undertook an extensive divestiture program. A third is W. R. Grace, which restructured itself.

What is especially striking about shrinking value creators is the extent to which the right answer for each involved shrinking in a way that restored the core business to its original status at the center. Consider Guinness, the Irish brewing business that stems back to 1759, when thirty-four-year-old Arthur Guinness leased a small disused brewery at St. James Gate on the outskirts of Dublin (at a rent of

£45 per year for a nine-thousand-year term). In 1886, Guinness became the first brewery to be listed on the London Stock Exchange, and soon after, it became the largest brewer in the world.

After World War II, the Guinness family launched a major diversification program, entering no fewer than 250 other businesses. By the early 1980s, Guinness's growth had ground to a halt, and its equity in Stout, the smooth dark beer for which it is famous, was severely eroded. The company's only hope was to retrace its steps back to the core. So it embarked on an aggressive divestiture program and, during one eighteen-month period, sold more than 150 of its businesses. The liberated cash was reinvested in the beer business to automate systems, develop new products, rebuild the Guinness brand equity, and fuel international expansion. Over the next eight years, the company's stock price increased nearly ten thousand times! Fortunately, Guinness returned to the profitable core before it was too late.

Exceptions to the Strong Core

This crystalline business form is a useful point of departure. Yet, while the data shows that market share dominance in a well-defined core business creates superior profitability, it does not address several more common situations.

First, it does not explain the success of many strong follower businesses such as American Express versus Visa in credit cards or Canon versus Xerox in copiers. Such an explanation requires a broader way of thinking about what types of market power and influence can achieve leadership economics without leading scale. The Internet is increasing the ways that follower companies can do that, while capital markets, which are transferring financial power to new entrants at many times their observed rate of production, are increasing the means for them to do so. Certainly, the ability of America Online to purchase Time Warner dramatically exemplifies that principle.

Second, while the data emphasizes the importance of relative market share in well-defined businesses, it does not address the increasingly common situation of blurred and fuzzy business boundaries that make it extremely difficult to determine market share and relevant competitors. Just think of markets such as communication lines into the home, in which cable competes with phone lines competing with wireless competing with T1 lines, and so on. No longer is it sufficient to keep track of only one set of similar competitors in a well-defined historical arena. No longer are you guaranteed a collegial industry association to collect and array market data, as was the case in industries such as steel and machine tools and typewriters. Today the equivalent industry association for each of these product groups would have ambiguous boundaries—if it existed.

The remainder of this chapter summarizes the key requirements for building a strong core as the foundation for growth strategy. For each, we provide some tools and suggest the most common sources of failure in the cases we studied.

Define the Business

Having a clear sense of business boundaries and of the definition of your core is a critical starting point for growth strategy. Are the boundaries stable or shifting? Which areas must be defended at all costs, and which are not strategic? From which areas will future profits likely spring, and from which will current profits likely diminish? What is the true source of differentiation and capability to win against competitors, and how might the shifting business boundaries demand changes in your core capabilities in order to compete in the future?

Perhaps the greatest danger in the companies we studied came from mistakes in business definition that led to premature departures from the core and misadventures in pursuit of businesses that should not have been pursued, and, in fact, whose pursuit imperiled the original core.

Dell Computer, the top performer of the decade from 1990 through 1999 among large companies, departed from its core with a jolt and quickly returned. Dell grew rapidly from its initial public offering in 1988. In 1993 it decided to expand from its core of direct sales of computers by launching a sales program targeted at discount retailers and wholesale clubs. Shortly thereafter, the company began to lose money. It suffered a loss of $37 million on sales of $600 million in the third quarter of 1993. Michael Dell and his team quickly diagnosed the problem as the company's departure from its core strategy and "direct sales model" and its attempt to sell just like its competitors, through retailers. Although the retail program constituted only 10 percent of Dell's business at the time, it had a huge effect. The expansion eroded the core itself because of, as Michael Dell says today, "the confusion [it] injected into our strategy. Every major business decision in the core business was set against the question of what it would do to the unprofitable retail part of the business. . . . When we realized this, we withdrew immediately. Even though it was painful and costly to do this, it was probably one of the defining moments for the company and saved us from disaster."[9]

J. Peterman wasn't so lucky.

The personal computer business in the early 1990s, the time of the Dell example, was growing at well over 20 percent each year and changing rapidly. It is no surprise that a small turn of the steering wheel could send the speeding vehicle of Dell briefly onto the shoulder of the road, shocking the driver into turning back onto the pavement. However, similar departures from the core can occur even in businesses that exist in much slower growth environments. No matter what your business or industry is, focusing on the core requires continual diligence.

The case of Hilti International provides a great example of the sustained, profitable growth that can emerge from refocusing on the core. Hilti was founded in 1941 by the brothers Martin and Eugen Hilti to commercialize their design of the DX nail gun for firing metal fasteners into concrete using a proprietary power-activated system. The company has since grown to nearly $1.8 billion as the leader in innovation in preformed drilling and fastening products.

During the early 1990s, Hilti found itself in an extended period of stagnant growth in an industry that has historically grown at less than 1 percent. The company responded by moving swiftly into a range of new products at the lower end of the market, including drill bits and fasteners, basic supplies, screws, and chemicals. This move brought an increase in revenue growth to 4 percent but also the unintended consequence of driving down profits and margins.

The Hilti family felt it was time for a more fundamental appraisal of its growth strategy. Examining every customer segment and product line in detail, management discovered that virtually all of the new lower-end products intended to increase sales per customer were unprofitable. It concluded that the company had moved prematurely away from its core competence of innovation in solving complex and specialized customer problems through new, highly engineered products and superior customer support. Indeed, a study at the University of Aachen during this time identified Hilti as being among the most innovative product companies in Southern Europe. For instance, Hilti developed the first drill with a vacuum surrounding its drill head to allow a mason to work without leaving a particle of dust on the floor.

Through initiatives of its CEO, Dr. Pius Baschera, Hilti refocused on its core. Baschera called the company's new strategy Champion 3C (for customer, competency, and concentration). The result was investment in product innovation and even deeper specialized application of drilling and fastening, such as diamond coring mining (strenuous applications with high-risk and demanding technical specifications) as well as new ranges of premium products, such as for wood working. At the same time, Hilti throttled back on the lower-end, marginal product lines. Its growth since the mid-1990s has been 9 percent in revenues and 14 percent in profits through increased geographic penetration and a burst of new technical products. One example is a small DX concrete fastener so strong that it can hold the weight of five cars after being fired by a gun into a concrete wall. Today the company is examining new growth initiatives once again. But this time, these extensions will cluster around the core of technical, highly engineered, premium products, leveraging the technical sales force and protecting the high-quality brand.

Setting the Right Boundaries

Without a clear point of view about business boundaries, it is difficult to determine competitive position, the relative importance of differently positioned competitors, or the relative strategic importance of different growth opportunities. To make the right decisions, it is critical to have a clear definition of your core business, the relevant business adjacencies that surround your core, and the competitive and economic landscape. The degree to which these adjacent areas are related to your own core is key to establishing your business offense and defense across the boundaries. Mapping out the territory should be the starting point of any growth strategy in business.

The profitable core is centered over your strongest position in terms of loyal customers, competitive advantage, unique skills, and the ability to earn profits. If you are not profitable in your core, except during the earliest phases of market development and startup, something is probably wrong. Surrounding the core are the most promising adjacencies for expansion, where the skills of the core can be leveraged or where defensive moves are critical to protect core customers. But these moves require a strong core to build upon.

But, you might ask, aren't we supposed to remove boundaries, not add them, to come up with growth strategy? Aren't we supposed to think outside of the box, not in and around a definition? No. Misdefining the business (whether through poor judgment or plain sloppiness) commits you to invest in areas unlikely to lead to profitable growth or to ignore areas you should reinforce. Defining the business accurately is a way of creating a logical hierarchy of territories in and around your core business that help you target wise investments, stop investments that are out of bounds, and track market share, making profit comparisons with competitors.

Just think for a moment of playing tennis. If two competitors had different definitions of the court but only one was right, the one with the wrong definition would surely lose the game. He would either fire shots outside the true boundaries or hit to a narrow space that was too small, making it easier for his opponent to return the ball. If a pair of doubles players had different concepts of the court boundaries, chaos would ensue, and the team would quickly dissolve.

Consider the following actual growth strategy decisions that hinge on subtle and difficult issues of business definition:

- Is Coca-Cola in the cola business, the soft drink business, the beverage business, or some other business? Ample evidence suggests that Coke has defined its business success as share of liquid consumed, not share of cola, and that this definition has enlarged the company's sense of full potential and emboldened its investment strategy ("I'd like to buy the world a Coke") relative to competitors.

- Is Marvel Enterprises, the creator of Spiderman and other characters, primarily in the comic book business, the superhero character business, the animation business, or the children's entertainment business? The answer has major implications for the management of character properties. Certainly, Disney chose entertainment long ago.

- Does the business definition of Amazon.com logically include just books and information, or does it extend to all consumer hard goods, all consumer retail on the Web, or something else? The company's expansion program is betting its future on a broad, and controversial, definition. Time will tell. One hopes that good work defining their business underlies the executives' choice.

- Does a glass windshield manufacturer correctly define its business as supplying windshields? Or should it consider creeping into subsystem integration, adding to the tasks it performs on and around a windshield or glass side panel? Consolidation is rampant in the automobile parts industry, with more and more companies integrating and assembling systems of doors, seats, or electrical subsystems and expanding along their value chain. Here, business definition has a defensive application as well as offensive.

- Are the new Internet exchanges, such as e-STEEL, in the exchange business, the software business, the Web-enablement business, or the value-added services (financing, logistics management) business—or are they application software providers? These issues will resolve themselves over the next few years, but today they are central to the growth strategy puzzles that confront executives in these new-to-the-world businesses.

- Is Nokia in the business of providing ever more sophisticated handsets, or can its hardware business shift to software and services embedded in the phone as a distribution vehicle? As the company's handset business starts to slow, Nokia must redefine its business in a realistic and attainable way.

- What must CBS do to strengthen its once nearly dominant core? Should it focus on content production; extend the core by creating and controlling the largest number of cable channels; reinvigorate CBS News to compete more vigorously with CNN, as NBC has tried to do through CNBC; or take some other tack? Which direction to choose?

- On an even larger scale, how should AT&T define its business now that the methods by which voice messages are transmitted change and the transmission of data (a much bigger slice of the telecom infrastructure) escalates and moves from traditional phone lines to wireless, cable, private systems, and, most of all, the Internet? What, then, are the business definition and the core of AT&T?

The need for a strong core business to support a growth strategy requires defining both what that business is and what it is not.

The Blurring of Business Boundaries

Without a clear and accurate point of view on the boundaries of your core business and how they might be changing over time, it is possible to make fatal growth-strategy mistakes. Throughout this book we caution that errors in defining a business are among the most frequent and most dangerous forms of strategic error. Yet today business boundaries are more difficult to determine and are changing more often than ever before.[10]

Our experience is that the size and scope of most core businesses that might establish significant competitive advantage are shrinking due to the use of outsourcing and customer segmentation specialists. At the same time, the area around any core business, the "adjacencies" of relevance for strategy, is growing substantially. Moreover, potential future competitors for your current core and future sources of control over the profitability (the "profit pool") in your core business lie in these adjacencies.

Consider the following examples. For years, digital imagery was a document management technology at the boundary of Xerox's core copier business. But it took the advent of high-speed printers, combined with the power of new word processing software, for digital imagery to become both a threat to and a primary shaper of the future profit pool for Xerox. Or consider network TV news, long a tight oligopoly of three participants, with cable TV at the fringes. Today, the three networks have a minority share of news-related programming viewed on television and an even smaller share of the margin pool. Or think about the dynamics in the telephone business today. At what point will wireless cellular services become the same business as land lines? When will Internet telephony emerge and affect the profit pools of both in a significant way? And what does all this mean to the definition of the telephone business?

These are three examples of large and increasingly important adjacencies around a once tightly defined core business. The blurring of boundaries and creation of larger arenas of relevance strategically around a core are being driven by a number of key trends that are likely to persist for the foreseeable future:

- Outsourcing and the disintegration of traditional value chains

- Increased customer microsegmentation and new, more narrowly focused competitors

- Increased competition among different business models rather than merely among versions of the same one

- Digital convergence blurring the boundaries between all information businesses

- Forces of globalization blurring regional geographic boundaries

- Increasingly sophisticated supply chain strategies causing competition between supply chains as much as between companies

Defining the Core

Your own core business is defined by that set of products, customer segments, and technologies with which you can build the greatest competitive advantage. Defining the boundaries is as much a matter of making sound business judgments as of applying formulas or doing calculations.

A critical ingredient in formulating the right business definition is a clear understanding of your core customers and products that are expected to yield a majority of profit economics, or that have produced those economics historically. We are surprised at how often we find that members of management teams, when interviewed one-on-one, differ in their opinions of the core customer set and products. Your understanding of and consensus about the core can be sharpened by analyzing profit numbers and by mapping out the profit pool for this core business across direct competitors and customer segments.

Once you have an understanding of the right economics of the core customers and products that you are currently serving, you can then examine successive segments of the market radiating out from that core. In some complex markets, there may be as many as ten total segments. Each must be understood and prioritized for resources. In general, we find that the key strategic decisions are made in the inner core and in one or two other segments emanating from it.

Taking the personal computer business as an example, think of the following distinct areas of economic activity, all related to competition and growth in companies such as Dell, Gateway, and Compaq. These segments are listed from within the core PC business to the farthest out from the core, as best as that sort of ordering is possible:

1. Segments within the core (PCs sold to elementary school students in the United States)

2. The inner core itself (the global PC market)

3. Indirect competitors for computing (such as dumb terminals attached to a network)

4. Enhanced PC products (such as low-end servers and workstations)

5. Potential future competitors (appliances and handheld devices)

6. Complementary products but different businesses (software, software loading, Internet service providers, peripherals)

7. Product line extensions (storage devices)

8. Upstream supply chain activities (components)

9. Downstream activities (retail, distribution)

10. Other businesses that could share costs with a PC business

Clearly, the majority of resources should be expended in defending and expanding the inner core of the PC business, in staving off new competitors at the boundaries, and in looking for complementary products and services to deepen customer relationships and increase spending per customer. However, it would be premature to define the business and develop strategy without considering the full profit pool of the PC industry, including supplier power, channel power, and the potential for new, disruptive technologies outside of traditional boundaries. Specific competitors might define their own inner core slightly differently, depending on their strengths. But the industry definition would be the same for all, emanating farther out into the list above (items 4 through 9). Apple, for instance, might define its inner core around educational applications, where it has its highest market share by far. Gateway might define its inner core by PCs sold to consumers as opposed to those sold to businesses, where it is much weaker.

Defining an area as noncore, at least for a while, can be as valuable as defining an area as core. By taking a competitive arena off of the agenda, you focus the organization and liberate attention and resources for the most important battles. Without such focus, organizations inherently tend to add segments and priorities. This is an especially costly tendency in successful businesses with a growing number of possible paths before them.

Defining the core obviously requires defining what is clearly irrelevant and what falls into the gray area that needs to be carefully monitored or anticipated. The key types of decisions that need to be anticipated in the gray areas, or so-called blurring boundaries, are these:

- Do I need to expand my definition to include a new segment or technology? If so, do I need to add it? If so, how?

- Are any of the competitive dynamics in the gray area likely to affect the profit pool in my core business? If so, how, and how should I react?

- Are any of the competitors that are not currently threatening likely to make incursions into my core customers? If so, what should I do?

- Are there capabilities or types of skills that I need to bring in-house now to be able to understand and, therefore, anticipate, some of the dynamics adjacent to my current core?

- Are there partnerships or alliances I could forge to insulate and stabilize my economic position surrounding my core?

Virtually every business has a core and an expanding and complex set of adjacencies. Defining the core is critical, but being extremely self-conscious and diligent about monitoring areas or competitors deemed temporarily to be noncore can be just as important to long-term, sustainable growth. As the examples and analyses in this book show, it is the balance between maintaining a strong core and adjusting to threats and opportunities in business adjacencies that is the central tension of growth strategy.

Differentiate for Unique Market Power and Influence

Successful differentiation creates lasting market power and influence over customers or competitors. This section discusses the traditional metric, relative market share, and then explores alternative sources of market power and influence, which sustained value creators are using to their benefit. The increasing potential for building substantial market power and influence in the absence of scale gives strong followers and new entrants a greater strategic edge than our data on stable industries might suggest, though they face a set of strict conditions for strong followership.

Traditional Measures and Sources of Market Power

Our data shows that in the decade from 1988 through 1998, approximately 75 percent of the sustained growth companies had achieved leadership in their core business, as measured by their market share relative to their next largest competitor. In spite of the current talk about "new business models," relative share is still the predominant source of market power. The original source of market power is not usually scale. Scale is a result of other forms of differentiation such as product development or channel control. In some sense, scale is an output of more fundamental competitive advantage in the core. Nonetheless, three-quarters of the most profitable companies in a competitive arena have superior relative market share. This differential drives, in most cases, superior cost and profits.

In an analysis of 180 companies across thirty-three industries, we determined the average rate of profitability over the cost of capital as compared to relative market share. We found consistently that the average returns for companies with weak relative market share (30 percent the size of the major competitor) was 21.6 points lower than for companies with relative market shares that were 200 percent of their major competitors. Although relative market share has been criticized recently in business writings for being used as the sole measure of market power and influence, it nonetheless remains a significant measure in a large percentage of industries.

Even in the Internet economy, we are aware of the intense day-to-day attention that many leading companies pay to relative market share, share trajectories, and relative share of the profit pool. This is true at EMC for gigabits of new storage by application versus the same for its major competitors. It is true at Dell Computer for new units sold by type and country. It is true at Microsoft for software installations of operating systems versus the same for, say, Linux. It is true at America Online for subscribers and for share of hours online. And it is true at Charles Schwab for tracking purchases of stocks online. In part this is because these measures now drive values in the capital markets, but it is also because they drive real costs and revenues.

Developing Market Power and Influence

In examining the source of market power for the top one hundred small companies as well as for a sample of our sustained value creators, we found four basic ways that companies acquire market power and influence in a competitive arena in a core business and thereby drive scale. These are arrayed in figure 2-2. All of these methods are available to all businesses—those that are followers and those that are leaders. A company considering its growth strategy should ask itself which of these is the true underlying source of power and influence.

Customer-Based	Channel-Based	Product- or Capability-Based	Capital-Based
• Superior service and relationship (loyalty) • High switching costs • Superior information on behavior/needs • Business model built around new segment	• Channel dominance • Partnership with leading channel participants • Control point in a network	• Low-cost production • Superior/unique features • New-to-world products • Patents • Deep share of wallet	• High valuation, creating acquisition currency • Capital availability, allowing companies to outinvest competitors

2-2 Companies Acquire Market Power and Influence in Many Ways

Customer Loyalty. The most robust form of market power derives from building a uniquely high and structurally stable level of loyalty in a well-defined customer segment. A mere 5 percent increase in the retention of a credit card company's best customers could lead to a value creation increase of 75 percent. This increase comes from extending the lifetime value from capturing a new customer and from realizing the permanent increase in growth rate from a change in retention and loyalty. Because increases in retention stop growth from "running out the bottom of the bucket," a growing company can magnify its rate of growth by 5 percent to 10 percent by effecting a permanent, one-time increase in retention. Few improvements in a business can have this impressive impact on sustained profitable growth.

Customer loyalty can be built as a competitive advantage in an existing customer segment, as USAA has done in the case of insuring the needs of current and former members of the military services. Today, USAA has over a 98 percent retention rate of this population and sells an average of 4.5 separate products to each of its customers, an almost unheard of share-of-wallet performance. USAA systematically tracks each customer through twenty-three life stages, carefully choreographing its marketing and sales programs around these events of greatest propensity to purchase.[11] The achievement of market power and influence through customer loyalty in these instances comes from switching cost to the customer in tandem with offering superb customer service and depth of knowledge.

The other way to build market power and influence through customer segment focus and loyalty is by identifying or even creating a totally new customer segment and dominating its experience of a product or service. Starbucks coffee grew during the 1990s at a 55 percent annual rate as compared with a mere 1.3 percent growth in coffee consumption. Starbucks serves eight million customers per week, who average an amazing eighteen visits per month to its stores. Customers commonly drive five miles to buy their cup of Starbucks coffee. On the surface, the pharmaceutical effect of the strong, rich brew seems an easy explanation for this loyalty. However, other companies' coffee is strong too. The lure comes from a carefully orchestrated combination of product, ambiance, and ubiquity. Certainly, many other companies, such as Nestlé, had the idea and the ability to develop a chain of coffee houses, but none used their leadership to do so. Starbucks' market power and influence is made potent by scale but did not begin with scale.

A survey of 2,116 online shoppers for apparel, groceries, and consumer electronics and appliances shows that customer loyalty and customer conversion rates are the two drivers of relative Web site performance. Each element is equally powerful over a year. Simulation of the long-term economics, however, shows that loyalty has the greater impact on the long-term customer base and on referrals to other customers. The longer they shop at a Web site, the more money customers spend. In apparel, for example, a shopper's fifth purchase is on average 40 percent higher than the first and the tenth is 81 percent higher than the first. And in terms of competition, those grocers, apparel retailers, and electronics vendors that built a core of loyal, high-return-rate shoppers achieved a competitive edge.[12] If anything, e-loyalty is even more powerful than offline loyalty.

To understand the power of loyalty consider this. We categorized the companies that our survey respondents visited according to their degree of financial success. Online apparel companies known to be performing well such as The Gap and Abercrombie & Fitch had retention rates nearly thirty points higher than those of the more poorly performing companies such as Alloy.com. Moreover, the better-performing companies had referral rates ranging from 30 percent to 70 percent, compared with rates of 0 percent to 10 percent in the worse-performing apparel companies. We went through the same exercise for consumer electronics, with the same results. The stronger companies such as Crutchfield had retention rates of over ninety, whereas weaker performers such as buy.com had retention rates ten points lower. Modeling the economics of two retailers, one with, say, twenty points more retention and, say, ten points more referral, shows a dramatic difference in the companies' financial performance. The results are clear: building deep loyalty in a focused customer segment almost always proves economically more valuable than building breadth without loyalty. Since our survey, some companies with retention and referral gaps relative to their competitors are struggling in the marketplace. Buy.com, for instance, was trading at a price of nearly $30 per share when it went public, shortly after our survey. Today the stock is trading for $3 per share.

Channel Dominance. Establishing leadership in a new or existing channel of product or service distribution is the second most common model of building market power and influence, sometimes from a position of followership. This is not a new discovery. It is how Venice transformed from a fishing village to the most wealthy city in Europe in the 1400s through its control of the channel by which spices and tea were then reaching the West.

Channel leadership is also how Dell Computer Company (the "growth stock of the decade" according to the *Wall Street Journal*) established its market power and drove to world leadership in PCs and workstations. Computer components, and even assembled computers, were available by mail order well before Dell was formed. However, no one saw the potential for the direct channel to gain share as clearly as Michael Dell did. Selling direct, rather than through layers of distributors, value-added resellers, and retail intermediaries (the way Compaq and IBM were selling their computers), had powerful economic advantages: lower cost due to fewer layers and middleman markups, lower pipeline inventory and fresher (higher-margin) components on average because of a six- versus seventy-day inventory pipeline, and a distribution channel tailored in cost and service to each customer segment. The brilliance of developing this channel was not only its lower cost but also its potential for higher customer service and, as luck would later have it, its ability to be turbocharged by the Internet. The natural structural advantage that this direct channel conferred was 10 percent to 15 percent over most competitors at one-tenth the inventory and capital levels. Today, 35 percent of computers are sold direct, and one day almost all computers could be sold through the direct channel. Other computer companies, such as Compaq, have tried to emulate the direct model that Dell pioneered but, so far, with limited success.

The Internet is providing many companies with the potential in their industry to enter and gain market power and influence in the new channel of online sales. Charles Schwab has used the Internet brilliantly to bootstrap itself from a follower in the securities and financial management market to consumers to the clear leader. We estimate that Schwab has three times relative market share of online trading volume and captures a hefty 70 percent of the online profit pool. Compare that with its share of profit in traditional channels, which we estimate to be about 12 percent.

There are literally hundreds of examples of new online consumer and industrial models for capturing the online channel for the flow of goods ordered remotely (such as Amazon), the flow of information over the Internet (such as Yahoo!), the flow of money or securities (e.g., Intuit), and the flow of industrial transactions (such as e-STEEL). All of these represent attempts to establish a lock on the control point for online users making purchase decisions.

Product Development Differentiation. The power of differentiation through superior product development is the rarest form of market power and influence in our sample of sustained value creators. Our analysis of the sustained value creators indicates that fewer than 5 percent rely primarily on this method. However, those companies that do build superior product development engines often are able to enter new markets, dominated by incumbents, and to gain market share profitably.

Perhaps the best and longest track record for building market power and influence through old products in new markets belongs to the Sony Corporation. Sony is now a $63 billion company that has grown revenues at a rate of 13.9 percent in 1996 through 1999 and profits at an astounding rate of 48.9 percent. It has a long history, since its founding in 1946 as a consumer electronics company, of growing by leveraging a stream of innovative products. Its first challenge, from cofounder Masaru Ibuka, was to create Japan's first pocket-sized radio. This deep and strong business core has remained and been adapted throughout the ensuing half century. For example, Sony entered the television business in 1968 and rapidly outgrew much larger competitors with its Trinitron televisions, due to their superior clarity and color quality. Today, the Sony TV is the standard of the industry. Another example: In 1995, Sony took on Sega and Nintendo in the home video game station market. Today, Sony is the leader in this market and has captured over 80 percent of the profit pool, with the next-generation version on its way. Sony is driving into the future by setting up a Computer Science Lab (in addition to its famed Sony Design Center of two hundred designers in eleven studios on four continents), which it claims will become bigger than Xerox PARC and is charged with examining how all Sony products can be interconnected in a single digital network. At the center of the company's remarkable record is speed to market, and at the center of that is fast prototyping.[13]

Capturing Capital. The capital market mania over the Internet brings us a final and dramatic way to capture market power and influence:

through establishing such a high market value, independent of market share and the profit pool, that massive investment and even acquisition are possible. And it is ultimately by deploying this "found" capital that companies establish market power and influence. Despite prominent coverage in the popular press, this is not the way most sustained, profitable growth arises. However, in selected competitive arenas, the capital markets have overruled the product markets in conferring power and influence on a challenger or on a first mover.

Even the battle among Internet start-ups sometimes becomes a race to the money. Critical Path and Mail.com are both providers of messaging and e-mail services. Today, both have sales of approximately $1 million and experience large losses. However, the financial similarity ends there. At its peak, Critical Path was valued at $3.2 billion versus Mail.com's $730 million. If Critical Path takes advantage of this difference in value quickly, it can propel itself to a much larger industry role through acquisition, just as Healtheon/WebMD did in health services and as America Online has in Internet access and content through its announced merger with Time Warner.

Seek the Full Potential Value of a Strong Core

Our argument so far can be summarized as follows: few companies grow and create value sustainably over periods even as short as ten years. Those that do so tend to focus on one, or at most two, core businesses in which they are clearly the leader or, in the rare cases of the strong followers, in which they manage to simulate the economic conditions that accrue to market leadership. These economic conditions and market power give companies higher profitability, greater control over the extended industry profit pool, and tighter control over investable capital in their competitive arenas. Typically, as in the obvious cases of Coca-Cola, Anheuser-Busch, Intel, and Microsoft, the continued application of economic leadership leads first to growth that outstrips that of others in the industry and then to "traditional" scale leadership. For instance, two-thirds of our sustained value creators grew more rapidly than their industry averages and were thereby gaining share in their marketplaces. In fact, the average sustained value creator in our database grew twice as rapidly as its industry in revenues and more than three times as rapidly in total profits. The question naturally arises, then, since most companies are followers, how can they gain market power and simulate leadership economics?

Throughout the discussions of sustained value creation, we have indicated our strong belief that many companies have, or once had, the right ingredients but somehow failed to recognize the potential of their profitable core. This failure has led companies to underinvest in the core, to set performance targets that are too low (leading to undermanagement), or to abandon the core prematurely for seemingly greener pastures in new or hotter industries. Companies consistently have a built-in bias, it seems, toward underestimating three dimensions of the core:

1. Increasing returns to leadership, leading to higher profits

2. Influence over investable funds, leading to competitive advantage

3. Influence over the extended industry profit pool, leading to access to superior profit growth opportunities in adjacent businesses

Increasing Returns to Market Leadership

How much should my business be earning? Where should I set profit and return on investment targets and expectations for management? These are critical questions that every CEO must answer every year. And many get the answers wrong by failing to recognize both the full potential of their core business and the potential for increasing returns on their investment in their core business's market position. In doing so, managers set targets that are too low, develop investment plans that are too modest, achieve growth that is too low, watch market share trajectories flatten, and give competitors incentive to invest more.

2-3 Market Leadership Drives Increasing Returns

Source: Data from 185 companies in 33 industries studied by Bain teams, including analytical determination of business definition.

Just how strong are increasing returns in the core? The answer varies by industry and competitive situation. However, the general pattern can be seen by returning to our cross-sectional database. Our findings, plotted in figure 2-3, indicate that companies near parity with their competitors earned a 14.3 percent return on capital. Market leaders, however, achieved a 22.1 percent return on capital, and strong market leaders saw that percentage rise to an impressive 25.4.

Clearly, a leader can earn ten to fifteen points or more above its industry average and gain market share at the same time. Dell Computer has earned a 200 percent return on capital while growing at a rate three to four times the industry average.

An example of a company that built an exceptionally strong leadership position and failed, for a time, to recognize its full profit potential is the Dun & Bradstreet Credit Services business. This business has roots in the early 1800s, when letters of reference from local bankers and prominent citizens such as clergymen were used to encourage businesspeople to extend credit to traders. The system worked well in small, local markets where community members knew each other, but as the U.S. economy grew, the method no longer sufficed. Moreover, the depression of 1837 saw more than six hundred banks fail, further heightening the anxiety of lenders and highlighting the need for a reliable method of establishing creditworthiness. Shortly thereafter, two companies were founded, R.G. Dun & Company and the John M. Bradstreet Company. For nearly a century these rivals skirmished, with both growing in tandem and suppressing the other's profitability so that neither gained a lasting competitive edge. In 1933, as the Great Depression came to a close, they merged to reverse their increasingly tenuous profit outlook.

Such was the core of the modern-day Dun & Bradstreet Corporation. The merger of coleaders quickly became profitable and prospered for the next fifty years. By 1980, the company's revenues were $1.2 billion, of which the credit business contributed about $500 million. This credit business, unlike its component parts of the earlier century, had a relative market share of more than six times that of its nearest commercial credit rival, had an 11.2 percent operating margin, and generated $56 million in profits, placing it well within the upper echelon of U.S. business performance. Yet, the following decade would prove that the business was still underperforming.

Under a new CEO and COO, the company reevaluated its credit business and concluded that this profitable core was operating below its full profit and growth potential. Over the next few years, the business increased its reinvestment rate, computerized its database, introduced new marketing concepts into its data packaging, increased its data quality and pricing, and added voice and online distribution services. By 1990, sales in the credit business had doubled to nearly $1 billion, the operating margin had expanded by nearly threefold to 28.2 percent, and profits had grown to $269 million. By 1997, the franchise had once again nearly doubled in revenues and profits.

What is important here is not the company's exact strategy but the amount of gold available to be mined in its core business with origins predating the Civil War. The Dun & Bradstreet case illustrates the hidden value of a strong core business and our strong but counterintuitive finding that the better performing your business, the more likely it is performing below its full potential.

Influencing Industry Reinvestment

Drilling down into twenty competitive pairings, we analyzed the extent to which our sustained value creators outinvest their competitors in their core business. We estimated reinvestment rate as the sum of capital expenditures, research and development, and advertising relative to sales. The sustained value creators invested at a rate of 15.3 percent, nearly twice that of their rivals, at 8.7 percent. Relative reinvestment is one reason that two-thirds of our sustained value creators grew at a significantly higher rate than their industry averages over the ten years we tracked. We find in our consulting work for large corporations that relative reinvestment rate is poorly tracked and analyzed, yet it embodies a great deal of information about an industry's future and competitive dynamics. Planning a strategy without collecting and interpreting competitor reinvestment rates is like forecasting the weather without looking at wind speed or temperature.

Consider the well-known case of Intel from the perspective of its historic focus on the core and relative reinvestment levels and rate. In 1980, Intel was smaller in total market value than either Advanced Micro Devices or National Semiconductor. Today, the company ships about twenty million units per quarter compared with its rivals' combined one to two million—a complete strategic reversal. And Intel's market value has grown to over fifty times that of the combined total of AMD and National Semiconductor. Since 1984, AMD and National Semiconductor have seen their stock prices rise and fall precipitously.

Part of the story is that over the past eighteen years, Intel narrowed its strategic focus and simultaneously adopted a preemptive reinvestment strategy. Intel, investing at the same rate as its rivals in 1984, narrowed its investment focus (from memory, chip sets, and integrated logic circuits down to just logic chips). It also turbocharged its rate of spending on new, low-cost manufacturing capacity and new products (such as the 486 family of chips). Its spending over that period ramped up from an average of $300 million per year to $2 billion per year by 1992 to more than $7 billion in 2000. By contrast, AMD and National Semiconductor's spending, as they fall farther behind, has hovered at $500 million to $1 billion per year.

Looking back, a former director of the Intel microprocessor business whom we interviewed, reflected:

> During the early 1980s, most semiconductor companies were trying to be all things to all people. We decided to take a different course, exiting the memory business and focusing all of our efforts on the development of digital logic chips for the PC. Our core investment principle became "It had to serve the mother ship," which was the microprocessor business, or it would not get funded. For the next fifteen years, we steadily ramped up our level of investment relative to competition while at the same time narrowing down, avoiding all diversification except that which clearly reinforced the core.[14]

The online investment advisor Motley Fool recently commented:

> Watching Intel and AMD [Advanced Micro Devices] battle is almost like watching the Harlem Globetrotters play the old Washington Generals. The Globetrotters (Intel) needed the Generals (AMD) in order to play the game (keep antitrust fears in check). The Globetrotters might have even made a match or two close to keep the spectators interested, but there was never much doubt who would end up winning the game.[15]

Influencing the Extended Industry Profit Pool

Every profitable core business can be thought of as situated at the center of a complex network connecting direct suppliers, suppliers'

suppliers, direct customers, customers' customers, complementary products, substitute products, competitors, and so on. Michael Porter has elegantly depicted these interconnections in many of his writings on strategy and positioning.[16] At the end of each of these economic connections is, usually, a pool of economic surplus and profit. The extent to which a company possesses the power of leadership in its core business influences the degree to which it can shape or even share in these profit pools adjacent to its own core business.

This concept may sound abstract, yet it is anything but. The recent government probes of Intel and Microsoft focus precisely on these companies' abilities to project market power in their core business to adjacent businesses (such as Internet browsers, in the case of Microsoft). The ripple effects that The Home Depot can project throughout its extended network of suppliers, and their suppliers, and their suppliers, are of primary strategic concern to those suppliers whose profits rise and fall with the moves and favor of a single customer. The ability of Coca-Cola to enter and influence, with ease, other soft drink categories—and maybe even the bottled water business—shows how leadership provides adjacent growth opportunities not as readily available to followers. Thus, the third hidden value of market leadership is the ability to shape the profit pool and to project its power and influence into attractive adjacent businesses.

Take the case of W. W. Grainger, a company founded in 1927 that has become the nation's leading business-to-business distributor of small parts and industrial supplies for maintenance and repair. Grainger offers over 200,000 products, from air circulators, engines, fans, and generators to hand tools and test instruments, to serve the needs of diverse markets, including commercial, industrial, contractor, and institutional customers. All products are available through online ordering or local branches. Grainger has 350 branches throughout the United States and Puerto Rico. In fact, 70 percent of all U.S. businesses are within twenty minutes of a Grainger branch.

Throughout the 1970s, Grainger grew profitably at 11 percent per year. Suddenly, in 1980, the business slowed to a 2 percent growth rate, which persisted to 1985. The attractive stock price growth of the company slumped, and profits per product in stock began to decline. At issue was whether Grainger—three to four times larger and more profitable than its nearest competitors—had hit the expansion limits of its industry. In its traditional markets, products, and geographies, its market share could be calculated to be as high as 40 percent. Moreover, industrial distribution businesses are notorious for being populated by mom-and-pop competitors that can operate on thin margins for a long time. Was Grainger's core business expansion over?

The company embarked on a major project to determine its full growth potential and barriers to achieving it. What it discovered was that it had misassessed the full potential of its core business by a factor of ten! What it had believed to be a $3 billion market for its core business was actually a $30 billion potential market. Grainger found that density of stores drove relative market share and profitability and that it could add many more stores in its traditional geographies. Adding stores lowered customers' travel time to the branches and dramatically increased sales. Moreover, Grainger had traditionally focused on specialized industrial buyers and specialized products— particularly electronics and electrical parts. Yet, the Grainger branch structure and customer name recognition of 85 percent could be parlayed into sales of a wider range of products to a wider range of customers, at a low incremental cost. The company could now sell a complete product line to its traditional core of customers. Together, the greater geographic density of stores and higher share of wallet lowered costs, increased the ability to invest in core customers, and improved service levels.

Grainger quickly identified and attacked its full-potential gaps with dramatic results. The company's revenues grew from $1.1 billion in 1985 to $4.8 billion in 1999, a rate of 11 percent, nearly twice the underlying industrial rate of growth for the basic supply products that Grainger sells. During this period, Grainger doubled its reinvestment rate and increased by a factor of ten the potential market its strong core business was going after.

Define the Profitable Core

In our experience, business definition is one of the most frustrating activities for senior executives. Although business leaders know that they should have a clear answer to the question, "What is our core business?" it is difficult to arrive at a fully satisfying statement. Part of the problem arises from blurring several distinct but related topics that need to be considered one at a time and then integrated in a consistent manner or within a single framework. In working toward a useful business definition, executives need to ask themselves the following questions:

1. What are the boundaries of the business in which I participate, where those boundaries are "natural" economic boundaries defined by customer needs and basic economics? What products, customers, channels, and competitors do these boundaries encompass?

2. What are the core skills and assets needed to compete effectively within that competitive arena?

3. What is my own core business as defined by those customers, products, technologies, and channels through which I can earn a return today and can compete effectively with my current resources?

4. What is the key differentiating factor that makes me unique to my core customers?

5. What are the adjacent areas around my core, and are the definitions of my business and my industry likely to shift, changing the competitive and customer landscape?

To illustrate the distinctness of these questions, consider a well-known business and product like Enterprise Rent-A-Car. The business in which Enterprise participates is the car rental market, including business, leisure, small-fleet leasing, and auto replacement in the event of an accident. Over the years, Avis and Hertz have also built up skills and assets in fleet management, reservations, pricing yield management, branch networking, and cost management that allow them to compete effectively in the rental car business. The core business of Enterprise, however, is probably the insurance replacement segment of the market, where it has over 70 percent market share and where its original business began and from which it is now branching out. The differentiators for Enterprise are its low-cost business system, its ability to work with insurance companies and body shops, and its ability to move cars and customers to each other. The adjacent areas around the core once included airport and leisure rentals and even leasing, but for a variety of structural reasons in the industry, these boundaries now seem to be blurring.

A similar logic can be followed in any business. Just think of some companies that you commonly encounter, such as McDonald's in fast foods or Blockbuster in video rentals, and play out the questions for yourself. None of them is easy to answer. All must be informed by answering the umbrella question, "What is my core business?"

Companies whose cores map perfectly to the "natural boundaries" of the business, that possess competitive advantage, and that are in an industry where the boundaries are not poised to change discontinuously are in great shape. Many of the companies in our list of sustained value creators fit this pattern, at least over the ten years that our data covers. Examples include Coca-Cola, Gillette, and Grainger. A more complex situation arises when the natural industry boundaries are quite different from a company's core business, creating either an unstable positioning or the need to develop a protected niche within a larger arena where larger companies prowl around the periphery of your core. One example is USAA in insurance, where the core is financial products for former military personnel and where the business thrives between behemoths such as Fidelity for investment and Allstate for insurance. Another is FootJoy in golf shoes, with Nike on one side and shoe companies on the other. A third is Porsche in automobiles, flanked by DaimlerChrysler on one side and Fiat on the other.

Conclusion

Achieving sustained and profitable growth is extremely difficult without having at least one strong and differentiated core business on which to build. The most enduring growth pattern is that of the strong, or dominant core business that benefits from continual reinvestment, constant adaptation to circumstances or business environment, and persistent leveraging into new markets or geographies, applications, or channels.

The three crucial first steps for a management team developing, refining, or reexamining its company's growth strategy are outlined in this chapter: (1) define the business boundaries and your own core business; (2) identify and verify the sources of differentiation that will continue to create market power and influence over your customers, competitors, and industry profit pool; and (3) comb through the core and assess whether it is operating at or near its full economic potential. Recall that the first paradox of growth is that the strongest core businesses are typically underperforming the most relative to their full potential.

3

The Alexander Problem

The tension between focusing on the core and setting out for new territory is universal and transcends business phenomena, spanning the affairs of nations to how to live one's life. The resolution of this tension is also the trigger point for the greatest blunders and most brilliant choices.

Alexander the Great ruled the largest area of the earth ever conquered by a single individual, stretching from Mount Olympus to Mount Everest. Although not everyone's idea of the model CEO, he amassed his kingdom in fewer than four years, covering over four thousand miles by foot, and winning 100 percent of his battles—a remarkable record in such a short time. But did he create *lasting* value? Just a few years after his death, his empire had dissolved and the captured territory slipped away. Alexander's problem was not inadequate initial resources or poor execution. It was the lack of a long-term strategy and the inability to exploit and consolidate his extraordinary short-term gains throughout the Near East to Nepal that stretched resources to govern too far beyond the Macedonian core.

His sticking point—the failure to anchor in the core business (in his case, governance) and consolidate a rapid expansion—exemplifies the most common problem across all growth strategy. Our analysis of the growth paths of sustained value creators compared with those of their competitors indicates that the selection of new business adjacencies around the core business is the decision that most often triggers either a new burst of profitable growth or distraction and stagnation. Embodied in this decision is a fundamental tension between protecting and investing in the core business, on the one hand, and expanding into adjacencies, on the other. The way companies resolve the tension often determines the sustainability of their growth.

This chapter focuses on the second element of our growth strategy, adjacency expansion from the core. We examine three topics critical to improving the odds of profitable, sustainable growth: (1) identifying adjacent business opportunities and recognizing the most common patterns, (2) assessing and choosing the right adjacencies, and (3) avoiding some common pitfalls of adjacency expansion. We also indicate how some typical views of adjacency expansion need to be adapted to today's turbulent business environment, with its increasingly blurred business boundaries.

Adjacency Expansion

Adjacency expansion is a company's continual moves into related segments or businesses that utilize and, usually, reinforce the strength of the profitable core. Over time, these sequenced moves can fundamentally redefine the core business (by adding new capabilities) as well as provide growth in themselves. Indeed, it is through adjacency expansion that a company in a stable industry repositions itself to go after the most attractive new profit pools or to respond to new environmental conditions.

Business adjacencies are growth opportunities that allow a company to extend the boundaries of its core business. What distinguishes an adjacency from another growth opportunity is the extent to which it draws on the customer relationships, technologies, or skills in the core business to build competitive advantage in a new, adjacent competitive arena. Examples of companies seizing adjacency opportunities range from Chrysler, moving aggressively into the minivan market, to Starbucks, selling coffee ice cream in supermarkets.

Many of the most successful companies that we describe throughout this book are in industries within which lie extremely rich adjacencies. Diagrams of the step-by-step growth patterns of these companies look like the concentric rings on the cross section of a decades-old tree. Adjacency-driven growth patterns are at the heart of the sustained, profitable growth of companies such as Motorola, ServiceMaster, Grainger, Microsoft, Intel, Dell, and Disney. Consider the following examples from American Express, Nike, and Dell.

American Express has grown by expanding its core business for more than 150 years. At the core of the original American Express company was a money order that could compete with the government's postal money order. The difficulty of extending this service into Europe spawned American Express's marquee product, the Travelers Cheque, in 1891. Travel-related payment systems have been at the heart of the company's adjacency expansion path through its launches of the American Express charge card in 1958 and the Optima revolving charge card in 1987 to the acquisition of more than forty-five hundred automated teller machines from Electronic Data Systems in 2000.

As with any 150-year growth record around a core business, not all has gone smoothly. American Express moved beyond its range of natural business adjacencies when it purchased Shearson Loeb Rhodes in 1981 and when it added Lehman Brothers investment banking house to the mix in 1984. One reporter said of this initiative, "After endless name changes and suffering the financial agonies of the damned, American Express decided to cut its losses and slink away. . . . American Express will have blown more than $1 billion, not to mention endless hours of management time and years of lost investment opportunities."[1]

Investors have supported the company's return to its core. Today, American Express is leading the charge online with its Blue card and is becoming the leading payment source online under its new CEO, Ken Chenault. The company, now with revenues of $19.5 billion, continues to grow profitably and sustainably at a 13 percent rate with 25.3 percent return on equity around its original core.

Now consider the strategy that Nike has used to achieve an average 40 percent compound rate of growth since its founding as Blue Ribbon Sports in 1964. Nike has not relied solely on the core for growth but rather has developed a strong core and then repeatedly reignited slowing growth by finding the next logical, large-scale adjacency in which to leverage its strengths.

Nike's growth pattern reflects successive and distinct waves of adjacency expansion. From 1976 to 1983, Nike focused on its running shoe core to grow sales at an annual rate of 80 percent. But the running shoe business slowed to zero growth, on average, from 1983 to 1987. In the next era, 1987 to 1991, Nike surged powerfully by extending its running franchise into new product segments, including clothing, and rekindled growth to 36 percent per year, only to slow to 8 percent in 1991 to 1994. From 1994 to 1997, the company refocused on its athletic shoe business with emphasis on celebrity endorsements, especially the Air Jordan line, and restimulated growth to over 30 percent per year. Since then, expansion has once again slowed, and the company is pursuing its next growth adjacency. Part of that adjacency will be in golf, epitomized by Tiger Woods's switch to the new Nike golf ball for the 2000 U.S. Open at Pebble Beach, California, which he won by a record fifteen strokes. Nike's up-and-down pattern is more extreme than the norm among our sustained value creators. However, it offers a striking example of how growth from the core can flag, thereby creating an urgent need to shift resources into nearby adjacencies.

Dell Computer's detailed growth path illustrates simultaneous expansion along multiple vectors: geography, products, customer segments, and ancillary services. The company began with direct phone sales of personal computers to medium-sized businesses in the United States. Since the early 1990s, it has expanded geographically to its present position as a fully global company with standard global products. It has expanded its products to increasingly highly engineered offerings, from PCs to laptops to workstations to servers to storage. It has also expanded into adjacent customer segments, from business to education to local government to multinationals, each segment served by a tailored and distinct selling protocol, cost structure, profit-and-loss profile, management team, and business model. It has expanded its ancillary services that ride along with the basic "boxes," from software loading to asset tagging to Internet services to consulting. Not all industries allow this logical, crystalline structure of adjacency expansion; the world is usually not so linear and geometric. However, in the case of Dell it was, propelling Dell to be dubbed the best performing company of the 1990s.

Expansion into logical adjacencies around a core business is an offensive strategy, but it also has defensive implications. Building a profitable cushion around your core business can help to keep new invaders away or to block a sequence of a competitor's moves that lead into your core. Microsoft's entry into the game console business against Sony and Sega was heralded by the popular press at the time as "a radical departure from its core business."[2] If the consoles were perceived as hardware products with game cartridges, this observation would certainly have been true. However, the Sony strategy in home networking includes positioning its PlayStation 2 product as a potential computing hub for the home. *Wired* calls PlayStation 2 "a platform so robust it may be all the computer some gamers and their families will ever need," describing it as a potential part of an array of home devices that "all talk to one another in a no-PC-required home network."[3] The challenges to realizing this potential primarily involve software, not hardware. And for that reason, not entering the home game console business would leave one of Microsoft's software flanks exposed to a dangerous new competitor.

Alexander Revisited

The tension between expanding the boundaries of a business, in the presence of success and seeming invincibility, and maintaining the original core is at the center of our earlier-described "Alexander problem." Alexander's string of victories, won by thinly stretched and tired troops traveling from Athens to India, is extraordinary. At each stage, his forces faced the choice to stop and consolidate or to press on into more and more distant and unfamiliar territory. They consistently chose the latter and appeared to have won. Yet did they really win?

Consider these examples of companies that pursued unfamiliar adjacencies and failed to turn back to their core business in time to avoid serious damage:

- In 1994, Quaker Oats attempted to build on its Gatorade drinks business by purchasing the sparkling fruit juice company Snapple for $1.7 billion. The result was major internal disruption for several years and the eventual resale of Snapple at a $1 billion loss. In reality, there was less synergy between Gatorade and Snapple than management had believed. The sparkling juice company constituted not an adjacency but a diversification.

- For a decade, the United Kingdom's National Westminster Bank expanded aggressively into the United States. But the bank encountered tougher U.S. competition than its executives had forecast. In the end, NatWest decided to sell its U.S. business to Fleet at a loss, not only having lost money in the United States but also having slowed progress in its core British market.

- In the 1980s, Saatchi & Saatchi embarked on a major program of buying professional service firms, consultancies, a public relations firm, and other supporting businesses in an attempt to create a "one-stop shopping" experience for its customers. But customers did not value Saatchi's bundling, and the company incurred seven years of losses. The expansion strategy constituted diversification, which destroyed value by causing a loss of focus on the core.

- Under new management and with a new growth strategy, Gucci drove aggressively into apparent product adjacencies in lower-priced canvas goods sold through mass channels such as department stores and duty-free shops. The company also licensed its name for products ranging from watches to perfumes. Sales grew, but profits collapsed. The Gucci brand eroded. The company had expanded into shallow profit pools and diluted its core franchise. Gucci finally returned to its core and pruned the new, unprofitable growth.

- In the 1980s, Anheuser-Busch bought Eagle Snacks in an apparently logical adjacency expansion. People eat snacks with beer. Some snacks are sold where beer is sold, and the same trucks could sometimes carry both. Yet these potential synergies never materialized. Frito-Lay controlled the profit pool in the salty-snacks business and, implicitly, in Eagle's profits. In 1997, having seen $120 million in cash flow out during a time that its core beer business was slowing too, Anheuser-Busch ended its adjacency misadventure by divesting Eagle to Frito-Lay.

Even the best companies continue to expand into unknown territory, despite mounting evidence of strategic and executional risks in so doing. And even great companies can lose their way in the midst of a hailstorm of possible adjacencies that pummel them with greater speed and power as the firms grow larger and more successful.

Mattel, for instance, decided to enter the software business in 1999, buying The Learning Company for $3.8 billion. At the time, The Learning Company was a strong, growing business that was the clear leader in educational software. Yet the investment community was skeptical. The Learning Company exhibited slowing growth, and its cash flow from operations had declined to negative $43 million. Mattel pressed ahead, saying, "We are truly excited about the benefits to be realized through the combination of our two great companies."[4] But software is in many ways a difficult business, and a true departure from the toy business. After the acquisition, The Learning Company's performance eroded to a quarterly after-tax loss of $100 million. Reporting on the aftermath, the *New York Times* said:

> Mattel's woes illustrate the obvious but often overlooked fact that not all corporate marriages are created equal. Some are wise; others are breathtakingly foolish. . . . With more mergers taking place—the dollar amount of combinations worldwide is up 24 percent from last year, according to Thomas Financial Securities Data—investors need to be on the lookout for disasters.[5]

Mattel announced its exit from the software business one year after entering it, selling it for a price of zero.

Another company with a mixed adjacency-expansion record is Gillette. Gillette is one of the great global brand names, having built a 70 percent market share and brand dominance in men's shaving products over the past century. The company began in 1895 with the concept of a disposable razor blade developed by a salesman named King Gillette, who lived in Brookline, Massachusetts. After six frustrating years of seeking funding for his venture, he combined forces with an MIT engineer and redesigned the product into what became the safety razor, which took off like a rocket around the revolutionary concept of safe self-shaving. The appearance in every World War II soldier's kit of the Gillette razor further propelled this product as the global standard.

Over the next fifty years, Gillette stayed relatively close to its core, adding new forms of shavers, shaving creams, and women's products. The past few decades, however, have seen the company reach out in many directions for new adjacencies, as its core shaving franchise captured such high market share that much of its growth had to come from the introduction of more elaborate systems like the Sensor, rather than from unit growth. Over time, Gillette added Braun electrical appliances (1967), Oral-B toothbrushes (1984), Parker Pen writing instruments (1992), and Duracell batteries (1996).

Some were justified by their impact on noncore businesses, where the acquisition was perceived to generate leadership in a new core area (adding Parker Pens to Waterman). Some were justified by the hope of leveraging the customer acceptance and infrastructure of the core toiletry franchise (Right Guard for men, Toni for women). Still others were justified more traditionally by their impact on the core business of shaving. For instance, in 1967 Gillette acquired Braun's small appliance business to help Gillette distribute its products better in international markets and to add Braun's electric "dry-shaver" technology to the Gillette product line. Braun has been a successful acquisition that has strengthened the core shaving franchise. Under Gillette's ownership, Braun has grown from $70 million of sales to over $1.7 billion and is now the second largest profit contributor, next to wet-shaving products. Interestingly, the core wet-shaving business plus the direct defensive and offensive acquisitions strongly related to the core account for virtually all of Gillette's corporate profit and new growth today.

From 1994 to 2000, razors and blades were still—nearly a century after its founding—the company's primary revenue and profit growth drivers, while pens, appliances, and toiletries showed negative growth in sales and declining profits. With a precipitous stock price decline and a call for refocus from its investors, Gillette is now divesting many of these noncore businesses and rededicating its resources to the core and the closer adjacencies. For instance, in August 2000 Gillette sold its "struggling stationery division" to Newell Rubbermaid Inc., saying "our resources will now be devoted to the three core businesses."[6]

Hewlett-Packard's Imaging and Printing Systems business is, on its own, a sustained growth company that has leveraged a strong original core, built in the 1980s, into a profitable $18.9 billion business today. Since 1984, the business has grown at an average annual rate of over 32 percent. In the past five years, revenues have grown at 9 percent and earnings at 14 percent annually. The past growth pattern and the future strategic road map of the business demonstrate the power of a strategy that leverages and continually strengthens its core to yield ever larger and more attractive adjacencies. Moreover, they show how a business with high market share can continue to grow by finding adjacencies.

The printing and imaging business had humble beginnings on some farmland in Boise, Idaho, when a manager in the computer peripherals business was given permission to develop a line of small, low-cost desktop printers using the Canon laser printing engine for one line (LaserJet) and the HP-developed new inkjet technology for the other (ThinkJet). With its combination of high resolution and low cost, this business took off during the 1980s, creating a strong core that persists today (its worldwide inkjet market share is 43 percent and laser printing share is 54 percent).

Hewlett-Packard has driven its growth through four types of adjacency expansion. The first, through the continual search for increasingly refined customer segments around which to tailor and focus its core product, is into new customer segments. One example is the large-format plotting business for architects. Leveraging its 72 percent market share in large-format printing, HP developed innovative inkjet technology that offered high resolution, high color fidelity, and color registration to graphic artists and quickly captured that market. Another customer segment is the home digital photographer, a segment growing over 300 percent annually, for which the company has developed a printer with embedded software that allows smart media cards to be inserted directly into the printer, rather than requiring decoding by a personal computer attached to the printer.

The second type of adjacency expansion, driven by technology adjacency and well-defined key customer needs, is into related product categories. A series of such moves has expanded Hewlett-Packard's business definition from printing to digital imaging. For example, as the graphic arts processes became increasingly digital, the company successfully entered the scanner market to better serve the needs of the graphic artist segment. It is now the number one supplier for all scanner segments. HP later combined the scanning technology with printing to create All-in-One Products (printer/scanner/fax) for the small office and Multifunction Printers (printer/copiers) for the office environment. These two new product categories have provided high relative growth in the past few years. Still another example is the entry into the digital camera business, an effort to provide customers with a completely integrated digital photography solution. From a cold start in 1997, Hewlett-Packard has become the number three digital camera vendor in the computer mass merchant channel within the United States.

The third type of expansion, through the search for more and more consumables and follow-on products for the core product lines, is into a broader range of printer supplies. For instance, HP has entered the branded paper market and attained a surprisingly high market share. One specific example is the company's line of specially treated glossy paper for use with home digital photography, which holds the number two market position and is growing rapidly with high margins. This "razor-blade" model has been central to the growth and profitability of all of the HP printers, especially the inkjet.

Finally, the fourth type of expansion, through reconceptualizing the printing and imaging marketplace in terms of the creating, printing and publishing of all documents, is into other copying and print processes. This move broadens the company's market from a $30 billion universe to a potential $130 billion one that includes newspapers, books, corporate central copying, and a variety of services for the home. One example is Hewlett-Packard's initiative to place printers throughout the home, either connected directly to the Internet or in devices such as set-top boxes, allowing everything from tickets ordered online to stamps to maps to advertising brochures to print from a TV console. Another example is a venture with Newspaper-Direct to enable the remote printing of newspapers at hotels, eliminating costly transportation and allowing visitors to get their local papers even when traveling on distant continents. While the "inner core" of this business will remain the small, low-cost printers in direct lineage from the original product launch in the 1980s, the outer bounds of the industry are being expanded and pursued in a classic way: obtaining growth and profits from the core creatively but without overreaching and weakening the core.

One final note on the HP printing and imaging business. The executive team is now describing the business's strategy and tracking and measuring both cash flows and investments in terms of specifically identified adjacent markets around the core. It has also developed internal reports to compare progress and investment in the core with those in the adjacencies.

We have catalogued case studies of hundreds of seemingly promising adjacency expansions that did not work out as forecast in financial plans. Indeed, almost every business executive has experienced adjacency expansion gone wrong. Venturing from the core is inherently risky. Yet if you are not venturing, and occasionally failing, you probably are not sufficiently pushing the boundaries. As Collins and Porras observe in *Built to Last,* "In examining the history of the visionary companies we were struck by how often they made some of their best moves not by detailed strategic planning, but rather by experimentation, trial and error, opportunism, and—quite literally—accident. . . . Opportunistic experimentation and purposeful accidents."[7] The authors go on to describe the expansions of Johnson & Johnson into baby powder, Marriott into airport services, and American Express into travel services, all unscripted successes. The company that does not have an organized way to experiment (General Electric refers to its experiments as setting up "popcorn stands") cannot reap the benefits of such "purposeful accidents."

Our intent in this chapter is not to pretend that we can offer a one-size-fits-all solution for deciding where to expand. What we can do, however, is suggest some methods for examining adjacencies that will improve the odds of making better decisions as well as raise warning flags on the most dangerous shoals that historically have shipwrecked the most growth strategies.

Defining and Mapping Adjacencies

It seems obvious that the stronger and more dynamic a company's core business, the broader its range of add-on expansion opportunities. It follows less obviously, however, that those companies with the strongest cores, and hence the most to sacrifice in losing focus, also suffer the greatest temptation to become distracted; they're confronted by the second paradox of growth. Therefore, companies trying to spring new growth out of a slowdown or to select new growth initiatives without jeopardizing a strong core can benefit from methodically inventorying and mapping out their adjacent opportunities.

The content for an adjacency map should come first from the opinions of the management team and then from employees in direct contact with customers, from outside observers of the company and its markets, and from study of the list of new businesses being funded by venture capitalists in related areas. At a recent executive conference, in fact, John Chambers of Cisco said that he carries around a card with the names of the twenty-five small company start-ups most relevant to his core businesses.

There are three basic types of adjacency expansion:

1. A direct move into an immediate opportunity. This is by far the largest category of adjacencies. One example is Staples's establishing Staples.com as a new channel to serve customers online. Another is Starbuck's decision to expand its chain of stores into a new geography such as China. A third is eBay's extension of its online auction franchise from consumer products to business products, a customer segment adjacency. And everywhere we see local restaurants offering a home delivery service, a simple product adjacency.

2. An "option" purchased in a business related to the core; a hedge against future uncertainties. Many of Intel's and Microsoft's venture capital investments in Internet companies could be considered more hedges against the future than immediate profit- or revenue-growth sources that reinforce the core.

3. A series of sequential moves that expand the boundaries and capabilities of the core business. An extreme example is WorldCom's decision to acquire MCI (long distance) and then add to that the acquisition of Sprint (wireless) to complement its position in cable and Internet services.

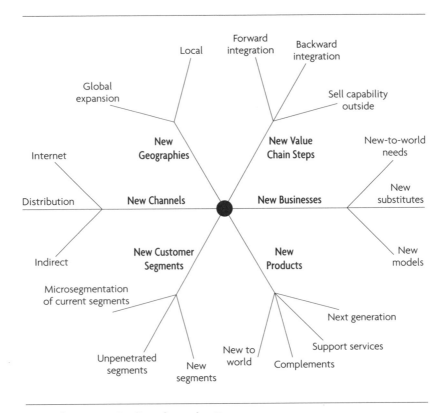

3-1 Adjacencies Radiate from the Core

Adjacency maps can reveal complexity of choice and trade-offs, as demonstrated by the map shown in figure 3-1. The choices are depicted as spokes leading out of the core business. One set of spokes and the branches off of it might represent customer segments where expansion possibilities reside. A second might represent new channels, a third new geographic areas, a fourth changes to the value chain, a fifth new businesses, and a sixth new products.

As another example, figure 3-2 shows a differently configured adjacency map, this one specifically for a company in the alcoholic beverages business. Along each spoke, opportunities radiate outward from the most to the least immediate extensions of the core business. It is possible, for a given strategy, to rank on the spokes those opportunities that are highest priority and those that are marginal.

3-2 The Multistep Adjacency Map of an Alcoholic Beverages Company

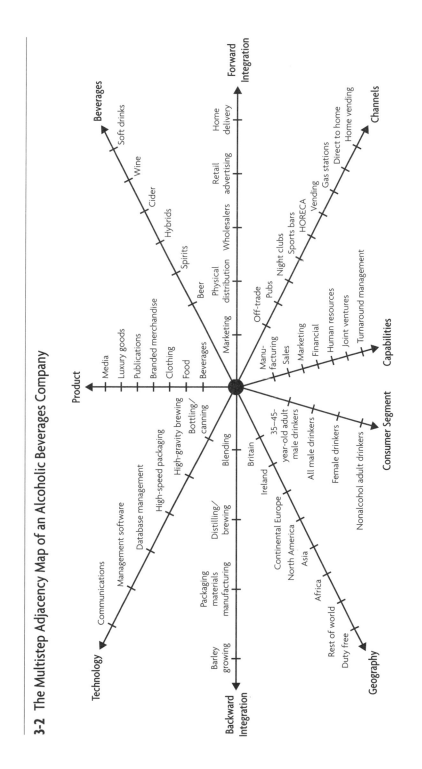

There are obviously many possible processes for mapping out and characterizing the full range of business adjacencies. Here is one that we have used productively. Begin by defining the core and gaining consensus about the most potent source of competitive differentiation and advantage. Having done that, identify and describe adjacencies step by step in the following order:

1. Identify the adjacencies you are in and array the data on how you are doing in each (market share, profitability, investment).

2. Identify the adjacencies your organization is considering or has rejected.

3. Identify other known adjacencies, including those that might require two or three strategic moves to reach.

4. Identify adjacencies suggested by your competitors' investment actions.

5. Identify adjacencies suggested by potential new competitors, often small companies.

6. Identify future adjacencies that may be created by technology or other developments.

7. Put all of these adjacencies onto a single grid or map (such as the maps shown in figures 3-1, 3-2, and 3-3), and push your thinking about what additional adjacencies might still be missing. A tool for doing this analysis can be found on the Internet at <www.profitfromthecore.com>.

Having developed an inventory of adjacencies and growth opportunities surrounding the core, do a quick ranking and rating of each. Such a ranking might be based on the following types of qualitative and quantitative measures: potential size, strength of advantage due to uniqueness of the core, strength of probable competition, offensive and defensive importance to the core (warding off invaders), a long-term perspective on multistep moves, and ability to implement. Forcing a ranking almost always stimulates a highly productive management discussion of core strategic issues grounded in data.

Finally, develop clusters of moves, or strategic scenarios, and do the tough financial and analytic work of developing your growth strategy. None of these activities is easy, but all are essential (in some form) for most businesses to engage in periodically.

As mentioned earlier, we are often struck by how many companies—from complex divisions of large corporations to small, early stage companies—do not look at their growth opportunities at the same time, in a strategic context, with a fact base to help support the priorities. The Bain annual survey of tools and techniques, conducted across a sample of 475 companies, provides corroborating evidence. In 2000, this survey found that "growth strategies" were the sixth-most-used tool, along with other standards like "pay-for-performance" systems and "customer satisfaction assessments," among the best-performing companies. By contrast, growth strategies didn't appear in the top ten techniques of the worst-performing companies. In a way, these companies are like people who are lost and neither have maps with them nor value carrying maps at all.

The process of mapping does more than just help organize opinions and inventory ideas. It reveals the extent to which the organization has a multiplicity of choices for growth and makes it easier to understand the trade-offs that may need to be made in choosing which to fund. In the absence of such a process, organizations often lack an agreed-on big-picture context for making decisions, fund an excessive number of initiatives to an insufficient extent, and take too seriously the "idea of the day."

Our experience and our review of sustained value creators show that a handful of most frequent adjacency expansion directions constitutes about 90 percent of the growth initiatives that are adjacent to a core business. The most common adjacencies to a core business are the following:

- Interlocking customer and product adjacencies

- Share-of-wallet adjacencies

- Capability adjacencies

- Network adjacencies

- New-to-the-world adjacencies

Interlocking Customer and Product Adjacencies

Perhaps the most common adjacency expansion is moving into new customer and product segments, using each move to reinforce the next. For some businesses, this approach to reinvesting has proven sufficient for decades of growth. It involves constantly adapting a product to enter a new customer segment and drawing on the knowledge gained about that customer segment to develop new product ideas that can then be applied in still other segments.

ServiceMaster has used this approach with great success. The company's origins trace to a 1930s mothproofing business run by Marion Wade, a former minor league baseball player who still dreamed of the big leagues. From there, it moved into carpet cleaning, riding the wave of postwar installation of wall-to-wall carpets throughout America. The company was named "ServiceMaster" in 1958 by Wade, a devout Christian who wanted to emphasize the importance of constantly serving the Master. The company's mission statement includes four commandments: (1) to honor God in all we do, (2) to help people develop, (3) to pursue excellence, and (4) to grow profitably.

ServiceMaster appears to have pursued its mission—certainly the fourth objective—well. Over the past forty years, it has grown by a compound annual rate of 21 percent and has consistently earned a return on equity of over 20 percent. In the past decade, it provided its investors an average annual return of over 34 percent, substantially higher than the rates of even the leading computer service businesses.

ServiceMaster's growth strategy has followed a consistent formula for over half a century, moving from one product segment into an adjacent product, then into a closely related customer segment, and so on. This growth is shown in figure 3-3 as a series of concentric rings representing growth into adjacent areas over successive periods

3-3 ServiceMaster Expands Its Services and Customers over Fifty Years

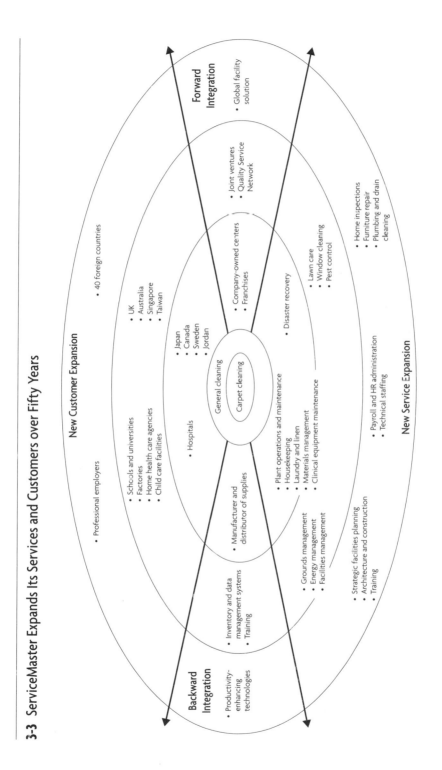

New Customer Expansion

Forward Integration
• Global facility solution

• 40 foreign countries

• Joint ventures
• Quality Service Network

• UK
• Australia
• Singapore
• Taiwan

• Japan
• Canada
• Sweden
• Jordan

• Company-owned centers
• Franchises

• Home inspections
• Furniture repair
• Plumbing and drain cleaning

• Schools and universities
• Factories
• Home health care agencies
• Child care facilities

• Hospitals

General cleaning

Carpet cleaning

• Disaster recovery

• Lawn care
• Window cleaning
• Pest control

• Professional employers

• Manufacturer and distributor of supplies

• Plant operations and maintenance
• Housekeeping
• Laundry and linen
• Materials management
• Clinical equipment maintenance

• Payroll and HR administration
• Technical staffing

Backward Integration
• Productivity-enhancing technologies

• Inventory and data management systems
• Training

• Grounds management
• Energy management
• Facilities management

• Strategic facilities planning
• Architecture and construction
• Training

New Service Expansion

of time. You can see the business expanding out from carpet cleaning to cleaning in general for residential and commercial businesses. General cleaning led the company in the 1960s to start cleaning hospitals (a suggestion made by a nun to the religious founder), where it also developed a grounds-management business. This new service then was sold to ServiceMaster's original segments of residential and commercial customers. Cleaning naturally led to laundry services. Grounds management led to pest control. This set of services led to a strategy to serve educational institutions. And so on, step by step, decade after decade.

ServiceMaster's growth has been more than 75 percent organic. However, the company has used acquisitions strategically to bring in new products and capabilities that are fully "plug compatible" with its core customers and that serve as catalysts for new growth. For example, in 1986, it acquired Terminix, the second-largest pest control agency in the United States, and leveraged its core customer base to achieve leadership in the new sector. In 1989, ServiceMaster acquired Merry Maids, a franchiser of professional maid services, which is now the leader in its business. In the 1990s, it purchased two lawn care operations, TruGreen and ChemLawn, which it consolidated and grew to create the leading lawn care business. Growth through pursuing close adjacencies, segment by segment, has proven a long-term formula for success for ServiceMaster.

A 1985 article about the company noted:

> A big numeral 2 rests on a cabinet in Pollard's [the president and CEO in 1985] office, under a wall full of co-workers' photos. It represents a goal of $2 billion in sales by 1990. Reminded that ServiceMaster hadn't reached $1 billion yet, and that its largest market recently got a lot tougher, Pollard replied with a grin, "Well, I like to make goals and beat 'em."[8]

And so he does. In 1999, ServiceMaster reported sales of $4.7 billion after another year of 20 percent growth—an increment of new, adjacency-driven business greater in size than the whole company was at the time of the 1985 interview. And in January 2000, Service-Master announced its next adjacency, WeServeHomes.com, in partnership with venture capital from Kleiner Perkins Caufield & Byers, which was to receive a 16 percent stake on its $15 million of investment. The new business is a tool to help customers manage their households and purchase home services.

De Beers is an example of a company that created growth for itself by helping its direct customers, jewelers, find new adjacencies to penetrate around their core business. One way was by using its marketing prowess to inextricably link its products with important occasions. De Beers's marketing efforts almost single-handedly turned wearing a diamond engagement ring into a cultural imperative in Japan, for instance. De Beers began its campaign in 1966, when the diamond engagement ring acquisition rate for all brides in Japan was 6 percent. By 1998, that rate had grown to 65 percent.

After the diamond engagement ring market was firmly established worldwide, De Beers reached out to a slightly older segment of women in a different geographic area with its promotion of the diamond anniversary band. From 1988 to 1999, the diamond anniversary band acquisition rate in the United States for all women on their tenth anniversary soared from 3 percent to 16 percent.

Most recently, De Beers used the millennium to its advantage. The company invested heavily in advertising, suggesting that the ultimate gift for the new millennium is a diamond. Sales in the first half of 2000 were up by 44 percent over the same period in 1999 due, in large part, to this initiative.

In addition, De Beers has shifted its focus to the diamond solitaire necklace in the United States, increasing sales from around $375 million in 1996 to $750 in 1998. It has also heavily promoted diamond ear studs in Japan, with equally dramatic results. In 2000, it moved on to its next product and is aggressively marketing the three-stone diamond ring.

Share-of-Wallet Adjacencies

A second strategy for growing beyond the initial boundaries of a core business is through moving into "share-of-wallet" adjacencies. By capturing most of the purchases your core customers make and then expanding their menu for purchases, it is possible to create a bond with your customers that substantially increases their loyalty. Such loyalty in the core customer base has several self-reinforcing economic consequences for strategy. First, it allows the cost of serving a customer to be spread across more purchases. Second, it increases both the retention rate and the life-cycle value of a customer. Third, it provides an opportunity to establish a deeper relationship with a customer, a by-product of which is more intimate knowledge of each other's businesses. Finally, it serves as a competitive deterrent, dramatically increasing switching costs. In some situations, doubling share of wallet can create a three- to four-times increase in profitability.

One of the clearest proofs of the lasting success of a share-of-wallet strategy is the Walt Disney Company's track record in expanding adjacencies from its core business with its deep roots in animated cartoons. The company began in 1923 as a partnership to develop animated cartoons. Its first product was a series of *Steamboat Willie* cartoons. In even this formative period of the company, the core of imaginative characters and application of the newest technical effect or innovation is apparent. *Steamboat Willie*, set to the music of "Turkey in the Straw," was the first cartoon to include synchronized sound. The most successful Disney products more than seventy years later, such as *Fantasia 2000*, remained strikingly similar. *Toy Story*, *Toy Story 2*, and *Dinosaur*, for example, were the first box-office hits to use computer animation throughout. Innovation punctuates the history of the Disney core, from the first full-color production to the first full-length animation, *Snow White and the Seven Dwarfs*, to the first integrated film and animation product, *Who Killed Roger Rabbit?*

In the early years, Disney's promotional skills and ability to find product adjacencies surrounding the core also became evident with the introduction of Mickey Mouse school writing tablets in 1929.

> These writing tablets were the beginning of the cross-pro-
> motion of Disney's cartoon characters that eventually
> made Walt Disney Productions a model of what business
> schools would later call "synergy.". . . Within three years,
> Ingersoll-Waterbury Co. was selling more than a million
> Mickey Mouse watches annually. Within a decade, ten per-
> cent of the company's revenues came from the royalties
> derived from the licensing of cartoon characters.[9]

Expanding these core assets, Disney marched into the construction of Disneyland in 1955 and into television with the companion
Disneyland and *Mickey Mouse Club* shows. Each adjacency begot
more related adjacencies. Disneyland sired Walt Disney World and
Epcot Center. The early licensing efforts parented a series of genera-
tions of now-familiar Disney products such as books, records, plush
characters, and magazines. These, in turn, spawned the chain of Disney Stores in 1987 and the hugely successful Disney Home Video
business that same year. Not all of Disney's expansions worked. One
restaurant initiative called Mickey's Kitchen was tried and abandoned. But the company was quick to experiment, and quick to stop
the losers and fund every aspect of the winners. Over time, the box-
office attendance of *Lion King,* for example, accounted for less than
20 percent of total profits from the film, with most of the profit pool
shifting into new adjacencies from videos to retail products to
Broadway adaptations.

Certainly, all has not been easy in the magic kingdom. Along the
way there have been major crises of leadership and family succession,
problems of cost overruns on projects such as Epcot, and problems
of being slow to adapt to the changing tastes of an increasingly
sophisticated child and teenage marketplace. Michael Eisner brilliantly addressed these problems, when he joined in 1984, focusing
on the untapped potential of the core asset of the film library and on
managing costs, productivity, and budgets.

Yet other problems of growth emerged, causing Disney to invest
in departures from the core. Desperately seeking a way to find the
next large wave of growth, Disney acquired sports teams (Anaheim

Angels and Mighty Ducks), media companies (Capital Cities/ABC), real estate ventures (time-sharing businesses), and magazine properties (Fairchild Publications). During this acquisition period, Disney stock languished and investors called for a return to core growth.

More recently, the company has pursued joint ventures that leverage the original core, such as its agreement with NTT DoCoMo to make the rich content of Disney available over the Internet in Japan in a variety of wireless environments. Today, these core-driven initiatives look promising, and Disney has entered an aggressive period of divestiture of noncore assets, stating, "We are not a conglomerate. If there are things that are maybe just off the core that we could monetize in a very strong economy, we may do that."[10]

The lessons from Disney are these. First, the original core can remain a source of adjacency growth for decades, if not longer, if managed properly and with adjacencies constantly monitored and assessed. Second, even the strongest core needs to be adapted in keeping with changes in its customer needs and technologies. Finally, even the most focused, excellent companies can choose adjacent moves that they later regret, only to return to the core.

At the opposite end of the glamour spectrum is Masland, a supplier of automotive interior systems, which used a different strategy to increase the share of wallet from its core customers. Masland was originally a supplier of floor mats, carpets, and other interior components to auto manufacturers. Looking to grow its business, the company studied its clients' needs and developed the goal of selling not individual components but integrated systems for the interior covering of a car, with parts drawn from multiple vendors. In fact, a wave of system integration is sweeping through the automotive market, a version of share-of-wallet strategy driven by the suppliers that assemble the subsystems of a car such as the door assembly, drive train, heating and cooling, wiring harnesses, and seating. Through consolidation and adjacency expansion, the number of automotive component suppliers has declined almost tenfold, from more than 3,000 in 1990 to only about 375 today, while the average size of supplier has increased from under $100 million to over $1.1 billion today. Some businesses have even been able to forward integrate directly into their customers' organizations. Grainger, for instance, now manages the tool room at many General Motors plants, and PPG Industries manages the paint line at some factories, including undercoat and cleanup.

The case of PHH Vehicle Management Services shows how a share-of-wallet adjacency can create profitable growth in a relatively basic and slow-growth industry. PHH is a leader in fleet leasing to large corporations, with a core business that extends back for nearly fifty years. Over the past five years, the company has turbocharged fleet leasing, a 7 percent growth business, by developing a range of supplementary services, such as maintenance services and accident services. For instance, it has assembled a nationwide network of repair shops qualified by a PHH expert. When a car in a fleet needs a repair and is taken to part of the PHH network, a PHH representative speaks with the repair mechanic to ensure that the right work is being done at the right price, given the company's extensive data-bank for benchmarks. Most PHH customers now sign on for this service, which only 15 percent took five years ago. PHH has found that its service adjacencies turn a profit, provide new growth, and deepen their customer relationships. It is now selling these services beyond its fleet customer base to businesses and individuals, creating another new adjacent growth source.

Consider yet another share-of-wallet example. The Boots Company is one of the United Kingdom's largest retail chains, with a brand name more trusted than the Royal Family, according to one source. Founded as an herbal remedy shop for the poor in 1849, it has lived a history of growth almost continually for 150 years, expanding into adjacencies of its original core medicinal dispensary. In 1989, in an aggressive move to obtain a higher share of its customers' wallets, it acquired Payless DIY and WH Smith's Do It All, merging these businesses to access the home do-it-yourself business.

As readers of this book might now expect, nine painful years and over $600 million of investments later, Boots sold its DIY chain at a large loss and returned to its core. A Boots spokesman commented,

"Our strategy has to be to differentiate the brand—we are not a health and beauty supermarket, we are a health and beauty expert."[11] Developing closer-in adjacencies in niche, health-related, higher-margin products and customer segments is now the more modest, and more profitable, goal.

With the amount of recent business analysis on the drivers of customer profitability and loyalty, the term *share of wallet* has moved into the common business lexicon. American Express has built the foundation of its cardmember strategy on adding services and increasing card flexibility to increase the share of wallet of its most profitable customer segments. Dell tracks its share of wallet for computer-related purchases of key segments and customers. The celebrated USAA business model is built on tracking a customer through his or her life cycle, aiming at maximizing the company's share of wallet at each stage. Industrial companies such as PPG Industries have developed programs around the full life-cycle use of their automotive coating products from priming to painting to cleanup to color-matching technologies for repairs of scratches. It bundles and sells products and services as integrated systems. The idea that new market share in the best customers is the most valuable of all is probably as old as business itself. What is new are our deeper understanding of the economic magnitude of share of wallet and our more sophisticated techniques for tracking and driving growth through share of wallet.

Capability Adjacencies

Capability adjacencies are moves outward from the core that are based on deep organizational know-how. In our sustained value creator companies, we have identified three forms of capability-based expansions. The first is grounded in technology or technical know-how. The second comes from business process know-how and the management model for running businesses. The third is founded on knowledge about how to store, manage, and obtain value from information, and the peculiar economics of doing so.

Motorola is one of the pioneers of wireless communications and technology and a great business-growth story of the end of the twentieth century. Though the company is currently addressing a slowdown in its growth rate, its longer-term record is exceptional. In 1979, Motorola was a $2.7 billion company with earnings of $154 million and market value of $1.6 billion. By 1995, the company had grown revenues ten times, earnings twelve times, and market value twenty-three times. Motorola's growth, which illustrates the first type of capability adjacency, derives from its deep skills in engineering wireless systems. Deep knowledge of wireless engineering, constantly refined, formed the backbone of Motorola for more than seventy years. Businesses where wireless system capability was not key to competitive advantage (such as automobile heaters) or where this capability conveyed declining competitive advantage (such as consumer televisions) were also those businesses where profitable growth was difficult to achieve or altogether nonexistent.

Motorola began in 1928 when the Galvin brothers, Paul and Joseph, purchased a battery eliminator business out of bankruptcy. Battery eliminators are devices that allowed early battery-powered radios to run on household current. This business quickly led the company into radios for consumer automobiles and police cruisers, a market that it dominated. During World War II, Motorola developed and produced the field radios, "walkie-talkies," that virtually became a symbol of the war and led to the firm's first public stock offering in 1943. During its growth, the company experimented with business adjacencies ranging from 8-track tape players to push-button gasoline car heaters, both of which failed. At the withdrawal of the heater product Paul Galvin announced: "We will now stick to electronics." Not a bad choice.

The adjacency expansion path of Motorola started in 1928 from the first battery eliminator. Since then, the company has built on its core wireless-engineering knowledge in essentially all of its successful adjacency expansions, including its forays into home radios, pagers, cellular phones, and the infrastructure for cellular phone systems. The success predictors of its expansions were the extent to which the core wireless technology was critical to the business and the extent to which market power and influence could be built on that technology.

Reuters is an example of a company that has leveraged information management expertise into adjacency growth with increasing success ever since Paul Julius Reuter first used pigeons to fly stock prices between Aachen and Brussels in 1851. Reuters has expanded its content over successive years to include news and a full range of financial and securities data worldwide. It pioneered the use of cutting-edge technologies to transmit such data.

For a company that has been in business since 1848, Reuters has done a wonderful job of maintaining a tight, well-focused core, almost like a cache of gunpowder waiting for the right spark to ignite profitable growth to a new level. That spark came in the form of the company's public offering in 1984, combined with the most modern technologies for transmitting and storing data. Consider the following: at the time of the public offering, Reuters had grown during its 136-year history to become a $360 million company with $45 million in earnings. In its next fifteen years, Reuters increased its revenues, earnings, and market value by fifteen times to become a $5 billion company with market value of over $15 billion. It followed a unique path in the way it leveraged information and in the knowledge of how to manage information, its core capability.

Reuters has grown in spurts by being quick to adopt new technologies for transmitting timely news and financial information, from the exploitation of telegraph services to the rapid use of the Dover-to-Calais cable to the first transatlantic cable to the telephone and Internet. An October 1850 description of the telegraph as "a portable machine which two people at opposite ends of the globe can use to communicate instantly with each other"[12] is remarkably similar to our characterization of Internet access devices today.

Leadership in the core is critical to Reuters's sustained profitability. Today, the company is the leading news and television agency worldwide as well as the leader in the provision of desktop financial information for securities analysts. Reuters embraced Internet technology at an early stage and is now the leader in supplying news and financial information to Internet companies. This leadership is the source of Reuters's 18 percent operating margins and high return on capital.

However, the company currently finds itself in the most turbulent operating environment of its life and faces a wide array of new competitors. Investor uncertainty has been reflected in its stock price. The recent slowdown, like others we have described in this chapter, is a common by-product of adjacency expansion in turbulent competitive environments.

Reuters is aggressively trying to expand into the U.S. market and into the delivery of information over the Internet. Its clear strategic intent is reflected in the rapid-fire alliances and acquisitions it has made over the past two years, including a joint venture with Dow Jones in interactive business data, a merger with Lipper in mutual fund tracking services, and acquisition of the trust analysis business of BT Alex. Brown. These adjacency expansions, farther from the core, build on core information management know-how. The trick will be to maintain core leadership while expanding into so many new adjacencies.

In their seminal article on core competence, C. K. Prahalad and Gary Hamel assert that many companies' growth strategies will "be judged on their ability to identify, cultivate, and exploit the core competencies that make growth possible—indeed, they'll have to rethink the concept of the corporation itself."[13] Prahalad and Hamel elaborate particularly on the examples of NEC and 3M, explaining that these companies have a strategic architecture that makes their competencies transparent and relevant in many settings. The cases of Reuters and Motorola, described above, illustrate extreme examples of companies whose profitable growth is a function of how they manage a relatively tightly defined set of capabilities into new business opportunities that surround the core. The tension lies between protecting the core (while not creating a static state) on the one hand and expanding into the right adjacencies (without abandoning the core) on the other.

Network Adjacencies

Robert Metcalfe, the developer of Ethernet technology and a student of networks, has observed that the power of an interconnected network rises geometrically with the number of users. The economics of networks in which the addition of a user increases the value of the network to all other users gives rise to increasing returns to scale and therefore to large rewards for network-dependent businesses that expand. Increasing returns create situations where incremental scale can be worth more to the leader than to other participants. This is why many software and communications businesses have characteristics of natural monopolies. Growth through incremental network expansion is valuable indeed for such companies. Economists have studied the competitive dynamics of networks extensively.[14]

For our purposes, many types of network adjacencies provide attractive growth opportunities for companies whose economics hinge on network effects. Perhaps the most obvious type is adding adjacent networks to a distribution or communications network. Consolidation of the railroads and, more recently, consolidation of cellular networks demonstrate this type of adjacency expansion, as does Vodafone's takeover of AirTouch in the United States and of Mannesmann in Germany.

Another type is accumulating groups of customers who can be put on a common information platform or service. Becoming the accepted standard for a consumer or business application software is of immense value. The growth strategies of Microsoft Office in desktop software, i2 Technologies in supply-chain management software, and America Online in optimizing its instant messenger software, AIM, all involve adjacency moves that are predicated on network economics.

The growth strategy of Jenzabar, the leading portal by which college students can communicate with each other and their teachers, consists of three prongs of network adjacency expansion. The first is adding new groups of users to the portal. The second is acquiring most of the major ERP software companies (Jenzabar has purchased five so far) that power the back offices of colleges, making Jenzabar the portal and platform of choice in these institutions, fully integrated into its other information technology functions. The third is adding services to the portal, such as travel-related services, that further magnifies its use and connectivity.

New-to-the-World Adjacencies

Just as volcanic disturbance can send new, and therefore uninhabited, land up from the ocean, so, too, can industry turbulence create new, uninhabited business territory. Often this territory comprises new-to-the-world businesses, and it can represent an important, opportunistic form of adjacency expansion.

Bain & Company is in the midst of pursuing one such adjacency. We discovered an increasing number of corporations struggling with the issue of how to obtain value from Internet-related ideas that draw on ideas or technologies in their core businesses but that are not necessarily appropriate to integrate within the core. Bain joined with venture capital firm Kleiner Perkins Caufield & Byers and with leveraged buyout firm Texas Pacific Group to create a new business called eVolution Global Partners, with the mission of helping companies create new business entities outside of their cores, as spin-offs. Several years ago, there was not a clear need for such a business. However, developments triggered by the Internet have made this an adjacency worthy of investment.

Cisco, one of our sustained value creators, found that many of its customers were asking whether it would be willing and able to transfer some of its business practices, especially those related to the use of the Internet and information technology, to help them transform their internal processes and become more efficient. Cisco has discovered that this consulting capability is not only valuable in itself as a business, but it can strengthen the company's core hardware business. As a result, Cisco is aggressively building this capability internally and through partnership investments such as its 10 percent stake in KPMG Consulting.

The Williams Companies, another of our sustained value creators, began in the early 1900s as a builder and operator of gas pipelines. In the 1980s, it recognized that the pipes and rights-of-way holding the gas lines could also be used for fiber-optic cables. Pursuing this white space adjacency, Williams installed and then sold its extensive fiber-optic network in 1995 to MCI WorldCom. Williams is now preparing to install even more advanced fiber in a 33,000-mile network called Williams Communications.

Evaluating Adjacency Expansion Opportunities

Management teams that develop a full inventory of growth opportunities and adjacency expansions around their core business(es) quickly recognize that they are awash in interesting and potentially attractive options for investment. Before they undertake a major data collection effort, they should step back and apply their strategic judgment and operating knowledge of the business to rate the opportunities along five key dimensions:

1. How much does this strengthen our core business franchise?

2. What are the chances of our becoming a leader in the new segment or business?

3. Could this move have a defensive benefit, preempting or interdicting our present or future competitors?

4. Does this investment position our core business strategically for an even stronger future adjacency, such as hedging against a major uncertainty or constituting one step in a well-defined sequence of strategic moves?

5. Can we be certain of superbly executing implementation?

We find that these questions provoke a rich and active discussion of priorities and lead to a second phase of prioritization of the activities that rate best. In general, if an opportunity fails on two dimensions, substantial questions should be raised about its attractiveness.

This second phase of prioritization can be more traditional and analytic, building a fact base on the following criteria:

- The size of the opportunity; that is, the current and future profit pool
- The strength of competitive activity
- Evidence about customer value and demand
- The magnitude and timing of investment
- The magnitude and timing of potential revenues and costs
- Uncertainties that could magnify or shrink the opportunity
- Difficulty rating of implementation

The final phase of ranking and selecting involves clustering the investment initiatives into distinct strategic scenarios. In one industrial company typical of many we have seen, the alternatives clustered into two scenarios. One option was built around a long list of initiatives for rejuvenating growth in a profitable but static core business. The initiatives included expanding internationally, forming smaller units for small customers, creating value-added services, providing information products, and developing new technology products. A second option entailed building mass and focus around several emerging customer segments. What began as an adjacency mapping exercise with more than ninety different ideas evolved into a highly productive strategic discussion about the future course of the business and where to deploy key financial, scientific, and management resources.

Mapping and ranking adjacencies can be as worthwhile for an early stage company as for a complex corporate division. David Friend, a professional serial entrepreneur, is now working on his fifth start-up. The pattern for each has been similar: build a technology with a range of customer applications, then choose and refine the customer focus as the launch date draws near. Friend's most recent company, eYak, is a bold, venture-capital-funded start-up that is constructing the largest, lowest cost, and most flexible telephone conferencing bridge in the world. The capabilities of the platform are sufficiently broad that a remarkable range of adjacencies surrounded its core platform technology (which itself could be sold as a business).

In fact, a systematic mapping revealed no fewer than twenty-eight adjacencies that could be justified and about which at least one person in the organization felt some passion. These opportunities were diverse and rich, from selling time on the Teleconference Bridge to developing a product for distance learning (with high-quality voice and Internet visuals). Once the adjacencies were mapped and prioritized, some of the alternatives were set aside for reasons of implementation, market size, speed to market, and competitive differentiation. The final list of four would have been difficult to achieve with a high degree of management consensus if the team hadn't undertaken such a fact-based development process in prioritizing the wide range of adjacencies surrounding eYak's core.

The logic for choosing a direction for growth is changing. Industry turbulence is both increasing the amount of uncertainty surrounding many choices and shortening the time frame for reaction. In addition, growth choices that were once primarily clustered in concentric circles around a core business (product choices, customer segment choices, geographic sequencing decisions) now include a much more vexing and fundamental set of adjacent opportunities (totally new businesses, hedging).

Furthermore, the cycle time of strategy development is becoming shorter and shorter in many industries. As a result, the evaluation exercise described above, which once might have been conducted annually (or less frequently) over a several-day period, now needs to be accelerated to quarterly, monthly, or weekly and compressed to a day.

Multiple-Move Adjacencies and Options

We argue throughout this book that industry structures are becoming less stable, leadership is becoming more fleeting, and the life span of a typical strategy is growing shorter. Risk and uncertainty loom increasingly larger in business life. In an environment like this, adjacency expansions are critical for staking your claim on future market positions as a hedge against uncertainty. The case for making these investments can sometimes be enhanced by going beyond basic net present value calculations and gut instinct to call on frameworks from options theory.[15]

Companies such as Intel, Microsoft, and Cisco use this investment strategy. As companies with extremely high market share in their profitable, core markets, they are aggressively seeking investments in adjacent markets and buying positions that hedge against a wide range of uncertainties, given the speed at which technology is moving.

Intel, for instance, has made more than 250 investments, totaling $3 billion, in companies, of which more than half are Internet start-ups. The rationales for these investments are both financial and strategic. On the financial front, *Red Herring Magazine* has tracked investments closely and reports, "The company's track record of Internet investment reads like a who's-who of the Internet. The company started making sizable Internet investments early in 1996, and those moves now appear considerably prescient as Intel emerges as a major shareholder in many of the leading Internet IPO's."[16]

Intel's investments in Internet content and e-commerce are also critical to its strategy for future sources of growth. First, Intel believes that because much of the future growth in chip sales is shifting to servers, rather than consumer-oriented PC's, the development of Internet capabilities and insight is a critical area in which to place bets, hedging against the future. In fact, in recent years Intel has spent more on these adjacency investments than on new chip capacity. Second, Intel's percentage of business conducted over the Web has increased in three years from zero to 42 percent in 1999. Third, the company is gaining an inside understanding of the new business models being developed because of the Internet. Bill Miller, the executive supervising the Internet investment strategy, says that "it should make us more nimble. It should make us a supplier of building blocks to the Internet. If we hadn't been making so many Internet investments, we wouldn't have been learning so much about the business."[17]

The lesson from this, and from a proliferating number of similar examples, is that adjacency expansions can and should hedge against future uncertainties and foster learning, as well as attack existing pools of nearby profit. Both moves are critical building blocks for a sustainable growth strategy.

Adjacencies and Choice of Core

The combination of a rich set of adjacencies and a strong or dominant core business can be a powerful breeder reactor for creating sustained, profitable growth if accompanied by appropriately aggressive reinvestment. Businesses with rich adjacencies around a weak core must first identify or create a strong core around which to build. Businesses with strong leadership but few logical adjacencies may need to redefine parts of their core (as discussed in chapter 4). More common are companies with multiple businesses, all funded in similar ways through the budgeting process yet all with different underlying positions and adjacency potential. In this situation, the richness of adjacencies around competing cores can be the deciding factor in determining how and where to focus a company and drive higher levels of growth.

Take the case of Oerlikon-Bührle (now renamed Unaxis). Oerlikon-Bührle was founded as a machine tool company in Switzerland in the early 1900s. By 1996, it was a CHF (Swiss franc) 3.9 billion conglomerate with holdings including shoes (Bally), aircraft (Pilatus), missiles, guns and satellites (Contraves), real estate, vacuum pumps and components (Leybold), and other sophisticated technology products including thin-film coatings (Balzers). From 1990 to 1997, the company grew at less than 1 percent annually with stagnant market value. A new board of directors and management team were brought in, early in 1998, to generate profitable growth.

Chairman and CEO Willy Kissling and his team evaluated all of their businesses and decided to narrow their focus around the core Balzers & Leopold subsidiary. Balzers & Leopold is the leader in many types of thin-film coatings for products ranging from high-wear metal parts to sophisticated optical sensors and memory devices. This division itself can trace its core business back to 1946, when Professor Max Auwarter built a factory, financed by the Prince of Liechtenstein, in two sheds in the town of Balzers to produce thin-film coatings. As time went on, Balzers attained leadership positions in one niche after another, today having captured more than 50 percent of the installed base of thin-film coatings. The adjacency map of coatings technologies in optical sensors and switches, memory devices, and semiconductors, mapped extensively by the CEO and his team, is especially attractive, showing many segments with high growth rates and deep potential pools of profit.

In only three years, the management team identified its area of focus and divested the company of nearly all of its other holdings. It then turned to strengthening and reinvesting in its core coatings business, investing in automation and streamlining activities. Today, it is ramping up investments to pursue some of the most promising adjacencies both organically and through acquisitions such as Esec and Plasmatherm in semiconductor coatings.

As of this writing, the stock price had grown from CHF 160 in the summer of 1998 to CHF 440. Revenue growth has increased to over 20 percent, even controlling for acquisitions, and analysts are predicting a continuation of that rate. Although the company shrank in total size, measured by sales, by 22 percent during the restructuring, it is now nearly three times as valuable as it was two years ago and five times as valuable as it was five years ago. Clearly, the new growth strategy of focusing on the strongest core and doubling growth investment in leadership positions with a rich set of surrounding adjacencies is working.

Common Pitfalls of Adjacency Expansion

Investment in adjacencies is eventually necessary for any company to continue creating value. It is also one of the riskiest activities a firm can undertake. In examining more than one hundred cases of business adjacency expansion, we have found seven primary pitfalls, or risk factors.

Pitfall 1: Expanding toward an Entrenched Position

Strategy, Liddell Hart's history of military strategy, examines the successes and failures of military campaigns to take over territory going back to the Peloponnesian Wars. Hart finds that armies that make a frontal assault on an entrenched position lose virtually 100 percent of the time, even with superior forces. He argues that an indirect approach is essential to increasing the odds of victory. For instance, Alexander's most decisive battle against the Persians, at Guagarela, was a masterful use of an indirect attack. In this battle, Alexander took a small fraction of his troops eighteen miles away from the front, attacking at an unexpected time from an unexpected direction while the majority of his troops were visible and immobile in the opposite direction. Alexander achieved an enormous psychological victory in addition to his military triumph. John Keegan writes that Alexander was "both outnumbered and irremediably overlapped, he had to devise a more subtle means to win victory." The indirect tactics he used "anticipated by 2,000 years the tactics that would make Frederick the Great the most celebrated soldier of his time." When the battle was over, Alexander had won decisively and "had established his authority over the whole of the empire and was poised to march 'to the end of the earth.'"[18] An analogous situation can be seen in business adjacency expansion. Launching a direct assault on entrenched positions, without a major new angle of attack or differentiation, seldom wins the war. Yet many companies try to move into adjacencies that are, in fact, the well-defended, entrenched positions of others.

One of Bain Capital's most successful investments was in Wesley-Jessen. Bain acquired the contact lens manufacturer for $6.4 million and took it public four years later to the tune of $290 million in equity, nearly a fifty times return. Bain saw a strong core (specialty lenses) underexploited because of a mistaken pattern of adjacency expansion. "W-J decided that it was going to move into the mass market for disposable contact lenses against Johnson & Johnson and Bausch & Lomb," explains Mitt Romney. "It built a $100 million factory to compete in this high-volume, low-cost segment and lost money every day doing that. In our opinion, W-J simply did not have the scale of the brand name to compete at the low end. This was a bad expansion strategy, too far from the core specialty segment where it was excellent. We saw this right away during due diligence. Our first action after the acquisition was to close the disposable plant and refocus on specialty."

Romney goes on: "The second phase was adopting a strategy that went back to the core. This had two elements. The first was what we called 'the forgotten doctor strategy,' to refocus on the most sophisticated fitters of lenses in segments like toric lenses for astigmatism. The second element was to take W-J's strong position in tinted and colored lenses and really drive this as a style product, with purple lenses targeted at U.S. teenagers, other colors targeted at the Japanese market, ultraviolet protection targeted at sports, and so on. This segmentation strategy building on the original core has been hugely successful in driving profitable growth."[19]

Pursuing areas of the market in which a company has relatively low odds of leadership or of building market power and influence can sap resources from the core and actually retard growth in the rest of the business.

Pitfall 2: Overestimating the Profit Pool

The odds of achieving success are much greater when growth goes after an expanding and deep industry profit pool rather than a shallow one. In their analysis of the Gucci example described earlier, Jim Gilbert and Orit Gadiesh write:

> Gucci's misstep highlights the problem with growth: the strategies businesses use to expand their top line often have the unintended consequence of eroding their bottom line.

Gucci attempted to extend its brand to gain sales—a common growth strategy—but ended up alienating its most profitable customer segments and attracting new segments that were less profitable. It was left with a larger set of customers, but a much less attractive customer mix.[20]

Mapping out the current and future profit pool is essential in developing a growth strategy. The profit pool is a function of potential market size and customer value from undertaking an activity. It is also a function of industry structure: the pool in a segment in which one participant can gain market power and influence is much larger than the pool in a segment that has multiple equal players.

Pitfall 3: False Bundling

If you flip through a pile of annual reports, you are sure to encounter at least a couple of phrases like the following: "Our aim is to serve all of the needs of our key customers." "We want to be the one-stop-shop for all of our customers' needs." In a few situations, this all-things-to-all-people approach might be appropriate. However, in general, phrases like these are warning signs of business boundaries that are too broad to be practical and that can lead to a dangerous overextension of resources.

One such example is the case of U.K.-based bookseller W. H. Smith. This highly recognizable book business, which caters to travelers, began in 1792 as a single new store near London and quickly expanded into newspaper distribution around London. Its bookstall expansion was fueled by the train traveler who needed not only newspapers but other goods for long trips on cold trains, including games, foot warmers, and even rugs. Today, W. H. Smith has over $3.5 billion in sales, a large distribution business, and well over one thousand stores of different types, still heavily catering to travelers.

Recently, however, with its core under attack from competitors like Dillon's and Waterstone's, W. H. Smith concluded that its problem was narrow participation in a broad retail space. The company began to fill that space by adding new retail product lines such as toys, typewriters, music, do-it-yourself tools, and gifts through its bookstores. The result was lower sales per square foot; higher costs in the form of inventory, infrastructure, and systems; and a management team distracted from defending the imperiled core of selling printed matter.

After losing £195 million ($310 million) in 1996, the board brought in new management with a new strategy: return to the original view of W. H. Smith's marketplace and business definition. Over the next two years, management dropped noncore products that had been added to the line and divested noncore acquisitions such as The Wall (a U.S. music retailer) and a majority stake in the Virgin Our Price megastore chain. It then used the money from these sales to reinforce and expand the core within the original business boundaries. In 1998, W. H. Smith purchased 230 U.K. news-stands from rival distributor John Menzies and began distributing its core products via the Internet. W. H. Smith still faces battles in a tough industry, but its gun sights are at least trained on the right battleground.

Some of the most well-documented examples of failed adjacency expansion are traceable to invalid assumptions about the economics of bundling. Allegis, the combination of United Airlines, Sheraton Hotels and Resorts, and Hertz predicated on offering the consumer a total travel package with a "one-stop shop," certainly illustrates a gigantic investment based on false expectations about consumer behavior. Similarly, Sears, in purchasing Coldwell Banker, Allstate Insurance Group, and Dean Witter Financial Services Group in order to offer its customers an integrated bundle of financial products, failed to realize that its department store customers simply weren't interested in the offering.

Pitfall 4: Invaders from Unexpected Fronts

The discovery of new, uninhabited market territory frequently brings invaders from unexpected directions. Consider the following:

- Kodak's pursuit of the digital camera market encounters unfamiliar competitors Hewlett-Packard and Canon

- Quaker Oats's attempt to expand Snapple beverages runs directly into new drink initiatives of Coca-Cola, with its unassailable distribution infrastructure

- Xerox's entry into low-end copiers gets a surprise attack from Canon, an unconventional competitor the giant had underestimated

Lacking familiarity with new competitors, companies tend to underestimate their strength, nature, and angle of attack. Instead, they need to x-ray every new competitor thoroughly to understand the world from that adversary's point of view, economics, and customers.

The exercise of mapping adjacencies requires not just taking an inside-out look at the market, but also taking an outside-in look at which companies might be amassing forces at your back. In an increasingly fast-moving and interdependent world, competitive blindsiding is becoming more common.

Pitfall 5: Failing to Consider All Adjacencies

The Massachusetts-based Polaroid Corporation was arguably one of America's first successful technology companies. Edwin Land retired from Polaroid second only to Thomas Edison in total lifetime scientific patents granted, a remarkable achievement. Yet, as the nature of film and imaging changed repeatedly, right up to today's digital imaging, the company remained fixed on instant (chemistry-based) photography. Even now, Polaroid's new product stream, led by a single-use camera called PotShots, is almost entirely based on Land's original core of patents and products. The company has failed to redraw its boundaries to account for the new, much broader, customer- and competitor-driven definition of imaging. Polaroid's business definition, instant photography, is driven by an internal point of view too narrow to lead to sustained, profitable growth. Its strategy based on this definition (and associated set of assets) has not been rewarded in the marketplace, as the stock price has dropped over the past five years by more than 50 percent in current dollars.

Companies like Polaroid, with a single, extremely strong product, historical technology, or long heritage of success in a protected niche, are the most vulnerable to drawing their business boundaries and list of options too narrowly. In these environments there are especially strong organizational and budgetary forces that can restrict business definitions. Narrow boundaries keep "apparent" market shares high, a crowd-pleaser to employees and analysts alike. Narrow boundaries provide psychological comfort and anaesthetize budget reviews. And, most important of all, narrow boundaries wall out the hard choices that may loom ahead.

Pitfall 6: Missing a New Segment

Failing to trace or pursue a newly emerging customer segment near your core can have lasting consequences. Consider, for example the case of rental cars.

Founded in the 1950s, the leading rental car companies, Avis, Hertz, and National Car Rental focused on serving the business traveler in the top one hundred airports in the United States. But the strategy issue for the rental car companies became more blurry as new segments sprung up and began to grow and take on a life of their own. The first new car rental segment to sprout was leisure travel. The second was the replacement rentals, serving drivers whose cars were in the shop for repair.

Alamo Rent a Car was founded by Florida entrepreneur Mike Eagan in1974, serving four locations with a fleet of one thousand cars. Alamo's formula was different because it was targeting a different population, the leisure market, paying for cars out of its own pocket. Eagan's model included lower-cost locations outside the airport, advertising focused at leisure destination and origin sites, and a dedicated sales force directed at travel agents and key influencers. Off-airport rentals are anathema to many time-sensitive business travelers on day trips, but they are perfect for the price-conscious family on vacation. Within fifteen years, Alamo had captured a leading share in the leisure segment and had grown its fleet to more than

150,000 cars, nearly 75 percent the size of the Hertz, Avis, and National fleets, on average. Alamo has since used its low-cost position to attack some segments of the business market, bringing it into much closer competition with the traditional airport-based rental companies that are now investing to move off of the airport sites.

As Alamo developed the leisure market, another company, Enterprise, developed the replacement market. In the 1960s, Enterprise's founders, the Taylor family, saw an opportunity to provide rental vehicles for motorists whose personal cars were unavailable due to accidents or repairs. Just as Alamo built a sales force presence in travel agents, so Enterprise invested to build a sales force presence at key body shops, insurance adjuster centers, and automobile dealers. These longer-term, even lower-cost rental needs required a different business model from Alamo's and a different business model from Hertz's or Avis's in terms of the condition of the cars, the size and quality of the locations, and staffing. In 1980, Enterprise had just 10,000 cars. Today, it has over 320,000 vehicles and has captured a commanding 70 percent of the replacement market, which it defined, created, and then dominated. It is now the most profitable major rental car company in terms of margin and return on capital.

Should the traditional rental car companies have pursued the leisure market more broadly during its early years of development, or the replacement market, or both? Would that have weakened their core airport business and allowed traditional competitors to make inroads? Or would early entry into leisure and replacement have been the winning strategy? Would the diversion of capital to develop these new businesses have sapped resources from more productive uses? Or would it have allowed them to strengthen their core by building a leading position in a new coalescing segment?

Pitfall 7: Single-mindedly Pursuing High-end Adjacencies

As Clayton Christensen has documented in *The Innovator's Dilemma,* in their pursuit of adjacency expansion, the strongest core businesses gravitate to the higher and higher ends of their markets, targeting more sophisticated products with higher margins that can support greater overhead. In the computer industry, for example, virtually every manufacturer of components and PCs has a growth plan skewed toward more sophisticated new applications or toward selling a larger and larger percentage of new product to the large corporate data centers.

The danger is that this approach may expose a flank at the low end to attack from new breeds of low-cost competitors. Examples of successful attacks in such situations abound, in industries from steel (Nucor) to brokerage (Schwab on line) to PCs (Dell). In selecting any growth strategy that expands into adjacencies, a company should ask itself whether it has avoided the low end of the market, and if so, why.

Containing the Risk of Dangerous Adjacencies: Diagnostic Questions

Clearly, the wrong choice or treatment of an adjacency expansion can do more than just lose money on that initiative; it can also distract core strategy, preoccupy management, and confuse investors with a multiplier effect to the detriment of all. There is no single formula for eliminating this risk. Indeed, bounded experimentation is at the head of the growth strategies of many of the companies that seem to expand rapidly from adjacency to adjacency, such as Sony or ServiceMaster or Dell or Schwab or Enron, and that have done so well. However, the risk can be managed.

In evaluating growth adjacencies, we have found a series of questions most useful in raising the right issues and, sometimes, clarifying the right answer. We recognize that many adjacencies fall into the close call area, especially where the future course of the marketplace is uncertain. However, even for those adjacencies, these questions can help to illuminate the nature of the risk and increase the possibility of lower-cost or lower-risk options.

To evaluate an adjacency investment, ask:

1. Does this adjacency strengthen or reinforce the core (or a core, if multiple cores exist)?

2. Does this adjacency add value for our core customers?

3. Does this adjacency serve as insulation against potential competitors intent on attacking the core?

4. Is this adjacency positioned in the direction that the industry profit pool (and the core) is likely to shift over time (growing segments, channels, needed capabilities)?

5. Do we have a chance of achieving leadership economics in this adjacency through outright leadership, a protected customer position, or shared economics with the original core?

6. Does this adjacency hedge against a major strategic uncertainty?

7. Does this adjacency lead to other successive moves that, in total, are essential to build or protect the core?

8. Does this adjacency move into the backyard of a new competitor? What might the competitor's response be, and how does that play out?

9. Does failure to move into this adjacency turn out to render the core vulnerable several moves down the road? To what degree?

10. Have we fully mapped out all the competing adjacencies, or are we acting opportunistically, without fully calibrating the options?

Few adjacencies will win uniform endorsement from the answers to all ten questions. If you have an answer to or a point of view about each question and their sum total encourages you to move ahead, then you should probably pursue that adjacency. However, if you have developed no answer to or point of view about some of these questions, then you need to probe more deeply. The riskier the decision, the greater the need to consider alternative strategies, such as participating in minority positions or alliances in order to hedge the risk.

To evaluate the method chosen, ask:

1. If achieving leadership would be difficult, does it make sense to enter this adjacency by ownership rather than outsourcing or partnership?

2. If uncertainty is massive, do the adjacencies that most hedge against the future require majority ownership, or is it possible to have several minority vehicles with options to buy later?

3. If the new territory is unfamiliar, what experiments or pilots could be run? Do those signal competitive intent and provoke response?

4. Who is the current leader in the adjacency? Does it make more sense to combine forces in some fashion than to add a new competitor to the arena?

Conclusion

The most successful sustained growth companies almost always follow the pattern of expanding in a regular and organized way into a series of adjacencies around one or two strong cores. The pattern resembles the growth rings of a tree, emanating out from the center, expanding and reinforcing the core.

Determining which adjacencies to pursue and how much to invest in them relative to the core ranks at the top of difficult and seminal decisions for any company in its quest for sustained growth. We have examined case after case of how management teams have overreached, undervalued their core in pursuit of far-reaching adjacencies (Bausch & Lomb, Gillette). We have seen examples of companies that have tentatively moved into important adjacencies, only to provide them too little management talent and too few financial resources. Often, these companies further endangered the core while pursuing less relevant business initiatives at the same time (Compaq, Polaroid). We have also looked at examples of companies that have been able to trigger wave after wave of new growth through an organized approach to resolving the tension between investing in the core and moving aggressively into adjacencies (the Hewlett-Packard printer business, ServiceMaster). Finally, we have seen cases of businesses that briefly departed from the core but that rushed back to reformulate the adjacency strategy in line with their true differentiation and turbocharged growth (Hilti, Dell).

Sophisticated management teams at the helms of all of these companies grappled mightily with the tension inherent in deciding whether to reinvest in the core, invest in adjacencies around the core, or consider hot new ideas that are distinct but that can build on strengths in the core. As their stories show, no one can bat one thousand. However, we hope that the examples, methods for mapping adjacencies, and diagnostic questions in this book will provide a useful framework for thinking about how to expand into the right adjacencies in the right way to gain full profit potential from the core.

The most successful companies have the largest number of new adjacencies raining down upon them every day. Success multiplies opportunities. Proliferating opportunities complicate decision making and prioritization (a good problem to have) and therefore risk. Paradoxically, the better your performance, the greater the risk in your decisions to select and invest in adjacencies around the core.

Of course, sometimes, the core itself encounters turbulence as technology changes or customer needs shift or a new business model appears on the horizon, gobbling up share in a surprising way. These situations are becoming increasingly common. Hence, we turn to our third element of growth strategy, redefining the core.

4

The Redefinition Dilemma

When naturalist Charles Darwin wrote of life on the Galapagos Islands in 1842, he noted an unusual strain of finch that had adapted to its environment to survive, and now looked and acted very differently from its continental cousins. These birds had elongated beaks that enabled them to eat local foods (insects, nuts, nectar from tropical fruits) that European finches didn't encounter. The evidence that a species had essentially redefined itself to successfully compete in a new environment became the cornerstone of Darwin's theory of evolution.[1] In the world of business, a similar evolution is taking place. Out of the turbulence in today's world, new environmental conditions are emerging, forcing companies to redefine themselves in order to survive.[2]

We have identified five main causes of industry turbulence. For example, the technology that allows telephone calls to be placed over the Internet at a cost of near zero is creating growing turbulence in the telecommunications industry. Information networking and retrieval software, such as Napster, quickly whipped up a hurricane in the music industry and, just two months later, in the film industry. A second is the emergence of a new, low-cost business model enabled by a variety of technologies coming together at the same time. The impact of retail superstores, such as Staples in office supplies and The

Home Depot in hardware, on local shops and department stores such as Sears illustrates this type of turbulence. A third cause is government regulation that suddenly increases or decreases competition. An example here, whose shock waves are still being felt today, is the U.S. government's deregulation of airlines. A fourth cause is a discontinuous change in the fundamental nature of customer demand and need driven by the customers themselves. The decision that Wal-Mart and other national chains made in 1994 to switch from local to national magazine distributors, for instance, precipitated a major price collapse and industry consolidation. Finally, the Internet is changing industry after industry from recorded music to securities.

The power of industry turbulence in determining winners and losers is apparent from a comparison of our sustained value creators over the past decade with the companies creating market value at the fastest rate in the last three years of that decade (not sustained value, necessarily, but created value). To examine this, we categorized the North American sustained value creators according to whether their primary growth engine was the historic core performance and adjacency expansion (such as ServiceMaster and General Electric), a new-to-the-world business model or market (such as Cisco and Dell), or a true transformation of a historic core (such as Schwab and Corning). Then we applied the same categories to the best-performing large North American companies. The comparison is shown in figure 4-1. Companies over the past decade, performing mostly before the turbulence of the last few years, grew and prospered primarily through core growth and adjacency expansion. In fact, 84 percent followed this traditional pattern. By contrast, companies that achieved the highest levels of performance from 1997 to 2000 were those that took advantage of turbulence to drive into a major new-to-the-world market, develop a totally new business model, or radically transform their core more rapidly than adjacency expansion would allow. In fact, over half of the best performers in that latter group were focused on new markets or forged from core redefinitions.

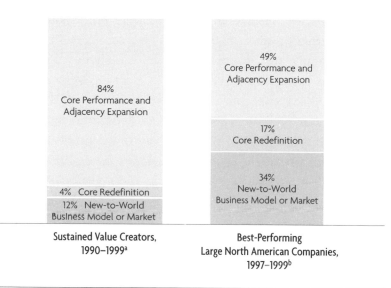

4-1 Turbulence Is Changing the Sources of Growth

[a]Based on sample of U.S. sustained value creators; $n = 67$.
[b]Large companies with highest three-year rate of value creation (through 12/31/99) as reported in the *Wall Street Journal*; $n = 35$.

An interesting and confirming study that examined one hundred new businesses from 1992 to 1997 found that fully 86 percent of the launches were essentially me-too businesses. The 14 percent that were genuinely new innovations garnered 38 percent of revenues and 61 percent of profits over the next few years, in part because they were better positioned to compete in new markets or expanding segments of markets.[3]

The Rarity of Successful Transformation

The need to redefine a core business fundamentally is becoming more critical and will become more common given the increasing frequency of industry turbulence. Yet history shows successful transformation to be quite rare. In examining our 240 sustained value creating companies' histories over the past decade, we found fewer than

30 companies that arguably underwent a major redefinition of their core business. We then conducted a search of other studies of successful business transformation of major companies in the past decade, scanned the business press, and reexamined our own archives. Even expanding the universe in this way to some 2,000 companies, we found fewer than 100 that transformed their cores fundamentally (with scale over $500 million). Indeed, in our literature search, about 15 common examples constituted most of the mentions of transformation. The most frequently cited of these companies include Corning, Charles Schwab, PerkinElmer Instruments, Nokia, Monsanto, Enron, General Electric, and The Williams Companies. Although we have not done an exhaustive population cohort study, it would seem that only about 5 percent to 10 percent of profitable and growing companies have transformed or redefined their core business fundamentally in the past decade. Given the deep roots that a company's historic core has, it is no wonder that change of this magnitude is seldom attempted or successful.

Because redefinitions come in all shapes and sizes, we needed a working definition. We decided that a company had redefined, or transformed, its core effectively if it was experiencing profitable growth and if it had changed its business model or its business definition fundamentally.

Not only were successful redefinitions of a core relatively rare (therefore a small sample to examine), they were extremely varied and situational. To get a sense of the range of transformations, consider the following four examples.

Seat Pagine Gialle: Shift to a New Business Model

In 1997, Seat Pagine Gialle was the organizational unit that managed the yellow pages business in Italy for the government-owned Telecom Italia. Three years later, after dramatic redefinition of its printed directory business, Seat-Tin.it had become one of the hottest Internet companies in Europe—effectively, the AOL of Italy.

The story of Seat's transformation begins with its privatization in October 1997, when it was acquired at a value of .35 euros per share by a group of industrial and financial investors. Lorenzo Pellicioli was appointed the new CEO upon privatization and quickly got to work strengthening and stabilizing the original core by building a new management team, developing a leaner corporate structure, reducing cost to double cash generation, and establishing the vision and the strategic plan to reshape the company from an inefficient province of the empire, filled with political appointments, to a powerful business. This process of strengthening the core took about eighteen months and included outsourcing manufacturing, restructuring the sales force (30 percent replaced, cost reduced 10 percent), automating the commercial process, establishing customer segmentation, developing differentiated marketing programs, and increasing prices (averaging 15 percent) in the least elastic product segments.

With a stabilized core, the company drove into six new adjacent businesses, including call center services, new directory services, and most important, the Internet. These new businesses are soon expected to generate two-thirds of Seat's revenues. The Internet campaign began with the acquisition of Matrix, the owner of three business lines: Virgilio, the number-one consumer portal in Italy; Active Advertising, the leader in online advertising sales; and Matrix.com, a leader in large Web design projects. In addition, the core yellow pages franchise was brought online, becoming a powerful e-commerce facility and a marketplace for small and medium-sized businesses.

Seat's stock price increased by twelve times to over 4 euros per share in three years. Although still in process, this transformation started with a high-cost, offline business that has become a leading information business and the premier business-to-business and business-to-consumer Internet company in Italy. This is a case of strengthening and shifting the center of gravity of the historic core business, following a new compelling vision and supplementing its capabilities organically and through key acquisitions.

Vodafone: Global-Scale Business Redefinition

Vodafone is the world's largest wireless telephone services provider, having knitted together major systems in the United Kingdom (Vodafone), the United States (AirTouch), and Germany (Mannesmann). The company is now on the brink of seizing the promise of the wireless Internet to transform its business model once again. In an astoundingly short time under the leadership of CEO Chris Gent, Vodafone has catapulted from a small regional U.K. carrier spun off by Racal Electronics (which viewed it as a noncore business) in 1991 to the fifth most valuable company in the world, with a market capitalization exceeding $300 billion.

The Vodafone story can be seen as a case of rapid adjacency expansion into new geographies (local to global) and services (portals and Internet services). However, the speed, power, and breadth of redefining a local wireless business are so breathtaking that it deserves inclusion in our list of successful redefinitions of a core business. Moreover, it was turbulence in the global market for wireless services driven by the movement to global standards, competitive merger threats, customer demand, and wireless license auctions that facilitated this redefinition of Vodafone's modest original local core.

General Dynamics: Shrink to Grow

General Dynamics was formed in 1952 through the combination of the Electric Boat Company, a builder of submarines and ships, and Convair, a maker of aircraft. The company grew rapidly during the defense buildup of the 1960s, growing its aerospace business and developing the controversial F 111 fighter. In 1976, General Dynamics purchased the Chrysler Defense business, and in 1986, it purchased Cessna Aircraft to become a far-flung defense systems conglomerate.

In the early 1990s, General Dynamics saw the impending defense cutbacks and recognized the danger of its participation across many businesses in which it was not the leader. Although the company had grown to over $10 billion in sales in 1990, it was about to lose money for the next three years. This crisis spurred new management to decide to reform around its strongest core business, marine systems, and to strengthen and broaden this core.

Over the next two years, General Dynamics shrunk by 70 percent, to $3.1 billion in sales in 1995, and returned to profitability in the process. With the proceeds from the sales in missile defense and aerospace, it acquired firms that reinforced and broadened the core, such as shipbuilder Bath Iron Works. These actions propelled the revenue of General Dynamics back to $9.0 billion with profits of $880 million. Investors responded well to the transformation of the company portfolio, pushing its market value from $1 billion at the start of the decade to nearly $12 billion at the end.

The casual observer of the General Dynamics story might see it as an example of a restructuring followed by renewed growth from a stronger core. And it certainly was that. However, it was much more. General Dynamics was among the first, in the late 1980s, to perceive the changing business model in military procurement. The fall of the Soviet Union and the dismantling of the Berlin Wall increased the pressure on defense spending. One consequence of this softening in military appropriations was the shift from cost-plus contracts, which had fueled the defense-oriented industrial establishment for decades, toward fixed-price contracts. These new contracts would put greater pressure on costs and profits. No longer would the government bear financial risk and fund growing capacity; now money would be made only by tight management of the backlog a very different business model. The management at General Dynamics felt that many of the company's businesses had, therefore, reached maximum value and that potential buyers (other defense companies) were enjoying the highest cash flow they would experience for some time to come. A Bain estimate of shareholder value created by General Dynamics five years after its restructuring suggests that one-third to one-half of the $9 billion value increase came from recognizing how the new rules of the game were going to shift value and acting accordingly, with swift divestitures and restructuring.

Enron: Shift the Core to Drive into New Adjacencies

Enron was created in 1985 by the merger of two natural gas companies situated in a relatively slow growth market. In the early 1990s, it began to experiment with selling financial vehicles to hedge the forward price of energy, a new and growing need triggered by industry turbulence. The early results were so encouraging that management moved seventy people from the core business into the unit and established an aggressive compensation plan tied to the performance of the new derivatives business. The profit potential and low asset intensity in derivatives and hedging instruments contrasted sharply with those of the natural gas business, encouraging Enron to seek out other adjacent opportunities to energy. Today the company sells more than six hundred permutations of its core financial instruments, including weather futures. Enron has become the leading trader in gas, electric power, paper, coal, plastics, and now bandwidth. For additional leverage and speed, Enron has been innovative in developing partnerships in specific product areas, such as with America Online and IBM in retail electricity trading and with Sun Microsystems in bandwidth trading.

In the ten years since its moves into the energy trading and derivatives business, Enron's revenues have grown from $4.6 billion to $40.1 billion, and its earnings have grown from $226 million to $957 million. Over 75 percent of its profits now come from trading, the new adjacent business that effectively shifted Enron's core. The company's performance, strategic focus, and new growth prospects have driven its market value up by a factor of nine times in nine years. The open-endedness of the trading platform for growth is apparent in Enron's new product markets, new forms of financial vehicles in those markets, and new geographies. For example, only now is Enron aggressively investing to grow in Europe and Japan.

As in the three cases above, Enron's incentive and ability to move into energy hedging were related to turbulent industry conditions in the energy-products market, especially the U.S. government's recent deregulation of the power utility industry. This deregulation effectively unbundled power distribution from energy production, allowing the formation of new markets for energy that now could flow more freely throughout the power grid in North America.

These four thumbnail sketches show how transformations vary along the following key dimensions:

- Method (organic versus discontinuous through acquisition)

- End result (shift versus redefine versus replace the original business model)

- Organizational structure of new core (integrated versus separate)

- Role of technology (limited versus decisive)

- Rationale (turnaround versus defensive versus offensive)

In a recent analysis of more than forty transformations, a Bain & Company team found that, beyond the obvious ingredients such as the "right strategy" or capability or resources, five key controllable variables drove success. These variables had strong statistical correlation with outcome and ultimate economic returns. In order of average importance, they were as follows: (1) time frame and sense of immediacy, (2) clear motivating rationale for the "point of arrival," (3) strong, committed, and visible CEO leadership, (4) strong economic stake in the result for management, and (5) willingness to change or replace management as necessary. Some of these findings, such as emphasis on a short time frame and willingness to destabilize the team, contradict perceived wisdom. All are echoed in the practices of the best private equity firms, many of which operate within tight time frames, as their holding periods are measured in years, not decades.

The Actuarial Tables of Corporate Mortality

Most biological species, including humans, achieve longer life spans with each successive generation. The opposite appears to be true for companies: corporate mortality and morbidity tables would show that companies' life spans are shortening and their health is more frequently imperiled, due largely to failure to adapt to rapidly changing environments.

In his work on the "living company," Arie de Geus assembled corporate population statistics suggesting that the average life expectancy of corporations in the Northern Hemisphere is well under twenty years. Only the large corporations he studied, which had started to expand after they survived high-risk infancy, continued to live on average another twenty to thirty years.[4] These findings are consistent with those of other studies of corporate life expectancy. For instance, the *Economist* cites statistics suggesting that the average European and Japanese company now survives fewer than thirteen years.[5]

De Geus also studies closely twenty-seven companies that survived more than one hundred years, led by Stora, the Swedish paper and chemical company that is more than seven hundred years old. In all cases, he found that longevity hinged on the companies' ability to transform their core business at a few critical times. In fact, de Geus found that all twenty-seven companies turned over their complete business portfolio, on average, at least once in their lifetime. Their ability to shift and migrate their core business, to adapt to their environment, ultimately determined their survival. As Charles Darwin said of species, "It is not the strongest species that survive, nor the most intelligent, but the ones most adaptive to change." The same appears true of companies.

The Increasing Odds of Corporate Morbidity

Every insurance actuary keeps not only mortality tables showing average life spans, but also morbidity tables showing rates of crippling injury and ill health. Much of our analysis reveals the large proportion of companies whose rate of return is—and has been for some time—less than their cost of capital. Many of them, such as

National Semiconductor, AT&T, Westinghouse, Sears, and Compaq Computer, are companies that once possessed the lion's share of value in their industry. Now they are seeing that pool of profits shift to new competitors and more adaptive historic rivals.

One measure of corporate morbidity might be the rate at which shareholder value is shifting. Whereas even a couple of decades ago company value moved like molasses, today it flows like quicksilver. Internet valuations in the late 1990s epitomize this trend. Consider the case of Amazon.com's analyst revaluation on December 16, 1998, when seventeen million shares were traded and the value of the online book retailer increased, in a single day, from $12 billion to $15 billion, an increment half the total valuation of offline market leader, Barnes & Noble. Barnes & Noble's counterattack led, five months later, to an initial public offering of its Internet division at a valuation of $3.2 billion. These almost instantaneous shifts in huge blocks of value are extreme, but illustrative.

Even apart from the volatile Internet-driven shifts in value, there is evidence that economic value vested in a leading company has grown more tenuous. Take, for example, the jockeying for position among the top three companies during the 1980s and 1990s in a sample of industries. Seventy-five percent of the industries we studied had increased rates of churn, which threatened or displaced the leader. The conclusion: leaders can lose position more easily than ever, and they do.

We also looked at the distribution of economic value across companies in these industries from the mid-1980s to today. Here, more than 70 percent of the total industry value (measured by share of total value) had changed hands or shifted across a wide range of industries, including health care providers, steel, computers, mobile phones, and mass retailing.

Most large companies are finding it increasingly difficult to maintain value. Half of the twenty most valuable companies in the United States, measured by market capitalization, in 1998 had not been on the list in 1988. A similar comparison of 1968 and 1958 shows an 85 percent overlap and suggests a three times more rapid churn rate today.

The Chances of Succeeding at Redefinition

The statistics on company life span and the rate at which leaders lose their place in times of turbulence provide stark evidence that redefining a strong core business is tricky. To gain greater insight into the odds of success and failure in business redefinition, we selected twenty companies that were leaders or strong performers in their core business and were profitable at the start of a period of turbulence in their industries. All twenty failed to seize the initiative to adapt and, as a result, performed worse after the turbulent period than before. Either new competitors emerged or strong followers took advantage of the leaders' inability to change fast enough.

This analysis included companies such as Digital Equipment Corporation and IBM (encountering the PC revolution), Tandy (encountering the information systems changes facilitating big-box retailers), McDonnell Douglas (encountering the rationalization of its core Defense Department customers), Xerox (encountering the radical shifts to digital information and networking), Kodak (encountering the entrance of a foreign competitor combined with the advent of digital imaging), and Delta Air Lines and United Airlines (encountering airline deregulation). Virtually none of our leaders improved their performance after the turbulence, despite an upswing in the macroeconomy worldwide. Rather, the financial returns to shareholders of these companies eroded by an average of more than ten points per year and moved from above to below the cost of capital!

Many companies that suddenly stall appear to have followed strategies that failed to recognize a need to redefine their core business or failed to act boldly once the need became obvious. Disney made this mistake before Michael Eisner took the helm as CEO. Or a company may expand aggressively into adjacencies when it really needs to continue to focus on repairing or strengthening its core. Our previously cited examples of Bausch & Lomb, Sears, and W. H. Smith illustrate this error.

The most devastating mismatch of strategy and growth cycle is found in the company that needs to redefine some fundamental aspects of its core business but instead, aware or unaware of the threat, continues to attempt expansion with its old model. Consider the following examples:

- Sears watched The Home Depot, with its low-cost and superior-service business model, sell hardware (the core of the Sears retail store) as it grew from one to ten to fifty to two hundred stores. Only when The Home Depot had become a $10 billion company did Sears began aggressively experimenting with alternative retail formats. But by then it was too late to stem the competition.

- Compaq conducted study after study that showed the superiority of using the direct channel, pioneered by Dell, to sell personal computers. And Compaq repeatedly announced that it was launching a direct initiative, or a new hybrid model. Yet, in spite of clear evidence that the direct model offered higher margins and potential to increase customer loyalty, Compaq has not been able to get direct sales off the ground and has lost leadership.

Redefinition Is about Speed

If speed were not an issue, core businesses could be continually repositioned through adjacency expansion as described in the previous chapter. However, when turbulence hits, typical organizational and strategic responses may not be fast enough for three reasons:

1. Major change programs that take too long to complete have a poor track record of results.

2. The capital markets penalize slow response to turbulence.

3. Slow response to turbulence can erode competitive position.

Lengthy change programs do not command organizational focus and attention. To understand this better, we examined twenty major transformation programs—both turnaround and new-growth strategies. The programs that were substantially completed in fewer than fifteen months yielded returns three times higher than the programs that took three years.

During the 1980s, reengineering caught corporate attention as a panacea to reverse slowing growth and fill emerging gaps in profit. Entire consulting firms rose and fell on the back of these major reengineering programs intended to transform corporations, eliminate layers, speed decision-making processes, and take advantage of new information technologies.

Reengineering attempted to make major change in core business processes done from the inside, rewiring the engine while it was functioning. Today the record shows that more than 70 percent of these programs were worthless or destroyed value and that many of the rest fell far short of their targets.[6] Indeed, even one of the early architects of the reengineering wave, Michael Hammer, has done research at the Center for Corporate Change that documents failure rates of this sort. John Kotter, at the Harvard Business School, has also studied more than 280 change programs and finds a failure rate of over 90 percent. The primary reasons for failure are a lack of urgency and of sustained energy and commitment to the required level of change once the difficulty and cost become apparent. This, of course, relates to time involved. In any organization, it is simply impossible to maintain a state of crisis and intensity over a period of two to three years. Yet the inherent complexity of reengineering made it difficult to implement large-scale programs in less time. The failure rate of reengineering was almost preordained by the basics of human behavior.

A second reason for speed today is to maximize market valuations. The capital markets reward first movers now more than ever before. In some Internet business situations, the capital markets are providing first movers such as America Online, Amazon.com, i2 Technologies, and Ariba the business equivalent of thermonuclear weapons: multibillion-dollar valuations and war chests to win top talent and strategic acquisitions. Although Merrill Lynch today has a trading Web site that is rated tops in the industry, the company suffered a major erosion in value relative to faster mover Charles Schwab. From early 1999, when online trading took off, Merrill Lynch's share price declined by over 35 percent in the next twelve months, while Schwab's grew by 40 percent.

The third reason for speed is to gain competitive preemption. Consider industries such as steel, automobiles, and electronic components, whose supply chains have the potential for major cost reduction using Internet-enabled techniques such as online exchanges and vendor management. Even if these supply chain initiatives will eventually reduce price levels and benefit the consumer without necessarily changing the size of the industry profit pool, the distribution of profits will shift the most rapidly to those who transform their business to use these new techniques first. For instance, Cisco has obtained nearly a 10 percent cost advantage over Nortel and Lucent in routers and switches by preemptively learning how to transform its business in this way. And in PCs, the contrast of high-cost Compaq with Dell is even more dramatic.

The continued struggles of sophisticated companies, such as Xerox, to transform their cores show how hard it is. Still, the hope and expectation that it will work appear to be fueling an enormous number of initiatives and experiments to create distinct organizations inside and outside of existing companies. Private equity is responding with vehicles ranging from incubators to new forms of joint venture between venture capitalists and corporations. It is as if the business community is trying all the latest body-building techniques to grow the management muscle required to redefine the core.

The rest of this chapter explores this phenomenon of redefinition and addresses three key questions:

1. How do I know when it may be time to redefine my core business?

2. What are the best organizational methods for tackling this difficult task?

3. What are the lessons learned from past successes and failures at redefining a core business?

When to Redefine the Core

Imagine senior executives' response to the following revelations:

- A large long-distance carrier, constantly claiming to its shareholders that Internet telephony was far in the future, discovers that quality is improving faster than expected and the reality of "free" long-distance phone calls is imminent.

- A large insurance company that knows all of its profits come from price variations and market imperfections in consumer knowledge sees a growing share of its customers pricing insurance on the Internet, exposing the company's price inefficiency to public view.

- A newspaper hovering near breakeven analyzes its declining classified advertising revenues and readership only to find that the shift to online advertising is under way and will accelerate in the next three years, draining the paper's coffers of revenue.

- A major automobile dealership discovers that its own original equipment manufacturer, with which it has had a forty-year history, is forming alliances to sell directly to consumers, and that its strategy is starting to work, threatening the very role of the dealer.

- A major bricks-and-mortar book retailer realizes that the 20 percent to 30 percent discount offered online is not a temporary phenomenon.

- An electronics components distributor that has been focusing on offering a full range of financial, logistics, and advisory services discovers that its new competitors are specialized firms unbundling these services using lower-cost online methods, and that its customers who prefer buying that way are starting to defect.

- A chain of retail stores devoted to selling shrink-wrapped software recognizes that the time is coming when most software will be delivered electronically or embedded in the next generation of computers.

These and thousands of other scenarios are illustrations of once-strong, focused core businesses recognizing the probable need to redefine their core in a fundamental way and grappling with how and when to do so.

Consider core redefinition in the case of Xerox. Xerox traces the roots of its core business back to electrophotography patents filed by Chester Carlson in the late 1930s. Trying to get his ideas funded, Carlson approached a long list of companies, including RCA, Remington Rand, General Electric, Kodak, and IBM. They all turned him down, content to stick with carbon paper. Subsequent decades would see the creation of Xerox and the gradual development of xerography up to the launch of the revolutionary 914 copier in 1959. This product transformed the copying industry, driving out of business more than thirty companies that primarily used mimeography, carbon paper, and diazo printing. The 914 truly detonated major industry turbulence—and growth. In the 1950s, offices in the United States made approximately 20 million copies, in tedious and slow ways. With Xerox machines, the number of copies exploded to 14 billion in 1966 and more than 700 billion by 1985.

For a time, Xerox held a virtual monopoly. But attacks from the bottom of the market by Japanese manufacturer Canon, followed by Minolta, Ricoh, and Sharp, triggered a decade of attack and counterattack by Xerox. From 1976 to 1982, Xerox saw its worldwide share of copier revenues decline from 82 percent to 40 percent.[7] Xerox's return to shareholders dropped to near breakeven. The company fought in the traditional manner of an awakened leader combating relatively traditional forms of competition in a well-defined business.

Today, digital technology is once again changing industry boundaries. Xerox machines now compete for share of document reproduction with more powerful faxes, high-speed printers connected to computers, scanners connected to printers, and e-mail. The convergence of technologies means that Xerox's key competitor may now be Hewlett-Packard in the broad arena of digital document management, a much expanded business definition. As a recent *Forbes* article commented:

The numbers tell an eloquent story. In 1990, Hewlett-Packard had $13 billion in sales and Xerox $18 billion. [Today HP has $47 billion in sales and Xerox has $19 billion.] While Xerox likes to speak of its judo strategy, its approach to the mass market for printers could less charitably be described as a catch-up strategy. It may work, but you don't earn HP-size profits by me-tooing.[8]

Today, Xerox is in the midst of major layoffs and divestitures of non-core assets in its continued and frustrated pursuit of redefinition from within.

Warning Signs of Industry Transformation

More passengers are killed or injured from turbulence in the air than from any other aviation hazard. With the exception of sudden wind shear, most turbulence can be seen and predicted with sophisticated Doppler radar detectors. Even wind shear instrumentation is developing rapidly. What are the warning signs for business of pending turbulence and the need to change course?

There are five key threats that should be tracked by the radar of companies that want to maintain profitable growth of a core business. In fact, our examination of twenty-five instances of turbulence (excluding Internet-related ones) that have played out over the past two decades indicates that the storm clouds on the horizon throw distinct, observable shadows at our feet. Advance warning of turbulence in each case was one of the following conditions.

Erosion of Low-end Product Segments. This turbulence starts, seemingly innocuously, with the washing away of market share of a low-end customer segment that was deemed unprofitable and difficult to serve. This is the "innovator's dilemma" written about by Clayton Christensen, where a new, disruptive technology with new, low-cost economics appears on the scene that makes the least profitable and desirable customers of the leader suddenly profitable and interesting to the new follower. By successively ceding low-end market segments, incumbents can back themselves into a corner. An example is the penetration of electronic trading in securities, a channel initially scorned by leading brokerage houses such as Bear Stearns and Merrill Lynch.

In the steel industry, these dynamics played out twice in rapid succession. In the 1980s came the entrance of low-cost Japanese steel manufactured by continuous casting. The Japanese, too, worked their way up the value chain in steel, starting with low-end commodity slabs and coils and moving to higher-margin product. Five years later, new competitors entered the industry, such as Nucor Corporation and Worthington Steel, both of which achieved lower costs in very small-scale production through minimill technology.

Erosion of Customer Segments. This form of turbulence first becomes apparent in increased customer defections. For example, consumers in the automobile industry indicate a 70 percent to 80 percent satisfaction rate with their cars. Yet more than half of car buyers switch brands at their next purchase. Satisfaction measures simply reflect customers' rationalizations of their past decisions. Defection or loyalty measures reflect consumers' actual behavior and reveal their true satisfaction. Loyalty data on consumers' reactions to small Japanese cars in the 1980s stands in stark contrast to the data from satisfaction surveys that anaesthetizes leaders, such as General Motors, to their untenable status quo strategy. Sudden changes in core defection rates spell trouble.

Erosion of Microsegments. One of the most corrosive dangers for a company is the emergence of a new competitor that can attack underserved microsegments of a customer base with a targeted and superior model. This danger is hard to detect and can signal a fundamental shift in the nature of competition. The Internet is sometimes credited primarily with revolutionizing commoditization and direct selling. In fact, the opposite is true. The Internet has laid slick tracks for microsegmentation and the emergence of true and more subtle product differentiation and customization. This means

Internet innovations often glide to market with a stealth that ambushes traditional competitors.

In the 1970s, ABC, CBS, and NBC accounted for 94 percent of the television viewing audience in the United States. Today, the combined network share of viewers is down to 27 percent. The difference is made up by hundreds of "narrowcasters," such as a golf station, CNN, ethnic stations, religious stations, science stations, sports stations, shopping stations, kids' stations, and so on. The great audience erosion from CBS News to CNN constitutes a microcosm of too-long-ignored opportunities unearthed by micro-segmentation.

Erosion of Traditional Business Boundaries.   Perhaps the most obvious, but also the most often denied, sign of change is the sudden erosion of traditional business boundaries, in effect doubling (or more) the number of competitors vying for a space. The advent of digital imagery, for instance, is a transformational threat to Xerox in the market for reproduction and to traditional film and camera manufacturers in the market for photography.

New Intermediaries and New Control Points.   Some of the most profitable businesses over time have been those that were able to control a position in a larger system that others needed to pass through, pass over, or use in some manner. Physical control points ranging from the Port of Venice, which controlled the ocean-borne spice trade to Europe in the 1400s, to the Panama Canal are physical examples. Electronic examples range from Microsoft's stranglehold over the personal computer industry by virtue of its proprietary DOS operating system to Ticketmaster's dominance in selling tickets to certain events online.

The profit potential of such control points—critical intermediaries on a journey or in a transaction or in a production process—explains the enormous burst of activity by venture capital–funded entrepreneurs to set up electronic exchanges. Examples are Houston Street for crude oil, eSTEEL for steel products, and Ventro for chemicals. If successful, these exchanges would become the virtual inter-mediaries across which massive amounts of transaction volume would flow. If that occurred, the exchanges could profit not only by charging transaction or subscription fees but also by selling other services (such as logistics or credit or data) at the point of sale. More-over, these exchanges would represent the standard for online trans-actions and could expand further into supporting software products. In mid-2000, a Bain & Company survey found that more than one thousand online exchanges were already functioning, nearly all of them having sprung up in response to the control-point opportunity within an eighteen-month period of time.

Internet-Induced Turbulence

The Internet is driving quick and dramatic change because it facili-tates lower transactions costs, distributes ubiquitous information, and enables the creation of networks. The Internet is creating struc-tural change in businesses with high information costs relative to total costs throughout the value chain, and with high potential for reducing transactions costs or obliterating unneeded steps. The impact of the Internet on company structure can be especially pro-found where there are many buyers and sellers, bringing communi-cations and network effects into play. A portfolio of businesses can be identified and categorized according to its areas for greatest Internet-induced change.

In one situation, the primary impact of change comes from new productivity sources. An example might be Cisco, the leading sup-plier of Internet equipment. Recognizing the business power of the Internet, Cisco quickly moved to transact 85 percent of its revenue over the Web. More important, the wide range of Internet-enabled productivity improvements has allowed the company to reduce its costs by $500 million. In software, Oracle is the leader in Web enable-ment and has reduced its costs by $1 billion. Companies that "Web enable" their core businesses first will be able to use the Internet to achieve substantial cost advantage over their competitors.

Most companies can profit from a second situation, where the Internet enables new growth from the core assets. U.S. West's yellow page advertising business benefited from such improvements. The company transformed its large field sales force from one solely focused on printed advertisements to one that also sells ads on the Internet and provides a substantial array of services and home-page assistance to small businesses. Already, this initiative has boosted the bottom line.

In the third situation, opportunities occur in business models where information costs are especially high. Examples include the distribution of books or electronic parts, in which search costs are large relative to the prices of the item and the customer and supplier bases are diffuse.

Litmus Tests for Redefinition

How do you know when it is time to decide whether a major redefinition of the core is in order? Charles Schwab determined that the current turbulence necessitates fundamentally redefining aspects of its core business once per year. Kodak committed several years ago to targeting half of its business from digital imagery and to making massive investments to enable it to do so. On the other hand, Sears watched The Home Depot "experiment" as it grew from one to ten to fifty to hundreds of stores before reacting. And Polaroid defended publicly its clinging to instant chemical-based photography as its stock price plummeted and investors called for strong action and redefinition. Yet prematurely abandoning the core or constantly creating false crises can be destabilizing to an organization. So, what do you do?

No single formula can be applied to these complex situations, but we have used the following litmus tests for determining when serious consideration of redefinition may be in order:

- Are top-tier venture capitalists funding businesses with the avowed intent of attacking a segment of your core business? If yes, drill down further.

- Are sophisticated recruits in interview discussions elsewhere in the industry asking tougher and tougher questions about your fundamental business model? If yes, assume they know something from their discussions.

- Is a new competitor beginning to gain surprisingly rapid market share in a marginal segment of your business that you once controlled? If yes, remember that many of the most disruptive technologies began to develop and spread in this way.

- Are steps in the value chain that you once considered core now being unbundled and controlled by specialists? If yes, then market power may shift to a player that captures and locks up a critical step, achieving a gatekeeper status to the rest of the industry.

- Are there fast-growing adjacent customer segments that you might once have been able to serve but that you could not now compete for without adding a new capability? If yes, then immediately study these customers and understand what is going on.

- Are there potential legal or regulatory changes that could eviscerate your competitive position in the core or your ability to compete for the next set of logical business adjacencies in your growth plan? If yes, then immediately formulate contingency plans to hedge against this uncertainty.

If the answer to two or more of the above questions is yes, the odds are that you should seriously consider realigning your core.

Preparing the Organization to Redefine the Core

Redefining a core business while still running it profitably poses several immediate and nontrivial dilemmas that are especially acute with many Internet-driven redefinitions:

- *Pricing.* To make the new model fully competitive requires developing different pricing strategies. But what does that do to the core business?

- *Staffing.* The new model of the core requires excellent managers to execute a difficult start-up and ensure that the company competes effectively. But the best managers are needed to run the original core, where all the profits come from historically.

- *Rewards.* The reward structure may need to be different in the newly redefined model. But how can all employees be motivated equitably?

- *Channels.* Selling a product in a way that competes with historic channel relationships is disorienting and difficult for the original core. But that core frequently holds the power.

- *Success.* Suppose that the new model is successful and begins to gain market share. What tensions does this cause during the transition phase, and can they be managed internally?

More than ever before, companies are grappling with the tension between redefining the core internally, to retain the value of one integrated business and set of customers, and redefining it externally, to allow independent strategies and attract the right kind of talent. Before launching into redefinition (assuming a concept of the new model and strategy), you must confront this choice and carefully work through its implications.

Waking Up to Core Redefinition

One day you wake up to discover that your core business will be at a severe disadvantage in the future because of changes in technology or customer needs or new competitive forces. Moreover, you find that these changes are occurring so rapidly that merely repositioning the core through either a series of adjacency moves or a limited acquisition is too slow a proposition. What is the best way, you ask yourself, to begin to reshape, or redefine, the core quickly while still making money in the original business in its original form?

First, identify which of three basic situations your company is in, as depicted in figure 4-2. The first is where a core business, serving a

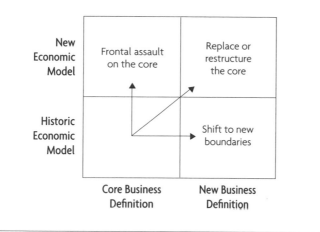

4-2 Companies Must Redefine Their Cores

core set of known customers, is confronted with a radically improved business model for serving its current core customers' needs. Examples of such "frontal assaults" on companies' cores abound. The emergence of Staples, with a cost model for delivering office products 15 percent lower than that of traditional stationers, is one. The rise of Dell Computer, with its direct model superiority over traditional suppliers such as Compaq, is another. Hewlett-Packard's use of low-cost, distributed printing of digitized documents, bypassing xerography, is a third. Still another is the emergence of Charles Schwab using online trading to displace competitors by doing trades at a fraction of the cost of a traditional transaction.

The second situation is where the original boundaries and structure of the core business are changing in complicated ways. An example of shifting boundaries is in the distribution business, where each step of distributors' once-integrated value chain (purchase, information, delivery, finance) is being unbundled and disintermediated. In maintenance, repair, and office supplies, for instance, Internet-based companies are now specializing in each step of the value chain. MRO.com will arrange and organize vendors, Credit.Com will provide credit, Aspect Communications will develop electronic business catalogs, and i2 Technologies will develop sophisticated supply chain software that companies can use to enable their own purchasing on the Web.

The third situation is where turbulence could remove the need for the core, thereby emasculating it over time. For instance, video rental stores, in the long term, face such a threat from on-demand electronic delivery of movies. At minimum, the rental segment will eventually shrink back to a small core that may have trouble supporting the current infrastructure of retail stores. Similarly, the manufacturers of large prop engines faced such a threat with the advent of jet engines. Polaroid, the leader in instant chemical photography, faces such a fate today in the face of instant digital photography.

The methods for fundamentally redefining a core business range broadly and are expanding all the time as the business community experiments with new ways to accomplish what was once a seldom-required initiative. Successful approaches include restructuring through divestiture, acquisition, or reverse merger as well as the more organic methods arrayed in figure 4-3, which spans the spectrum from changing the core processes from within to spinning off a new core into a separate company with professional outside investors. Figure 4-4 summarizes the trade-offs between integration and separation.

We have been involved with numerous clients wrestling with these trade-offs and have seen situations where each has been judged to be on the right or the wrong path to redefinition, given their specific time pressures and competitive threats.

Situation 1: Frontal Assault on the Core Business Model

The primary considerations in mobilizing your Internet response to an assault on your core are speed, cannibalization of the core, and long-term reintegration imperatives with the core business. There is no single best answer for all cases. For instance, one study that focused on the telecom, photonics, and computer hardware industry found that willingness to set up structures that cannibalize the core

4-3 Methods for Redefining the Core Lie along a Spectrum

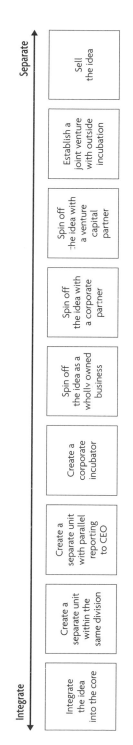

Integrate

| Integrate the idea into the core | Create a separate unit within the same division | Create a separate unit with parallel reporting to CEO | Create a corporate incubator | Spin off the idea as a wholly owned business | Spin off the idea with a corporate partner | Spin off the idea with a venture capital partner | Establish a joint venture with outside incubation | Sell the idea |

Separate

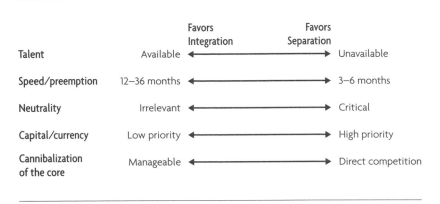

		Favors Integration		Favors Separation	
Talent	Available	←		→	Unavailable
Speed/preemption	12–36 months	←		→	3–6 months
Neutrality	Irrelevant	←		→	Critical
Capital/currency	Low priority	←		→	High priority
Cannibalization of the core	Manageable	←		→	Direct competition

4-4 Redefining the Core Involves Making Trade-offs

business in an orderly manner was the differentiator between companies that successfully navigated through turbulence and those that didn't.[9]

Consider the case of DoveBid. DoveBid was founded in 1937 in Foster City, California, by the grandfather of the current CEO, Ross Dove. It was an auction business that focused primarily on excess inventory or salvage products from businesses. During the 1984 to 1986 downturn, the company acquired new customers: it began to auction off computer inventories in Silicon Valley, still using its historic, live, fast-talking, "open outcry" auctioneering. This core business served the family well, with few adjustments needed, for more than fifty years. However, in 1998 that changed.

The success of eBay in consumer auctions, combined with the early emergence of online business auction start-ups, impelled Ross and Kirk Dove to investigate the feasibility of taking their business model online. They decided to launch an initiative integrated throughout the company; if it worked, they would go public with a redefined core that prominently featured Internet-enabled auctions. They raised $4 million from Freemont Ventures, the venture capital arm of Bechtel, and developed their plan in the spring of 1999. The new business initiative immediately took off, requiring two more rounds of venture financing during the year from blue-chip investors such as the Mayfield Fund, Softbank Group, Texas Pacific Group, Comdisco, Yahoo!, and Sun.

In just eighteen months, DoveBid's online revenues have grown to nearly half of all of the company's winning bids. DoveBid has developed an integrated hybrid model in which the live auctions (that you can hear on the Web site) blend bids from the Internet and the audience. It has used the funding to further expand its hybrid, clicks-and-mortar strategy by buying the largest U.S. business-salvage auction house, Robert Levy, as well as three brokers and an appraisal company. Powered by the Internet strategy, the company has more than tripled in size in a year, not including the acquisitions, and is preparing for an initial public offering.

This is a case where speed was of the essence because online competitors, such as TradeOut, had mobilized. It is also a situation where the economics demanded that the online offering be fully integrated with the offline to most effectively manage the auctions. Moreover, a true integrated hybrid model had even better projected costs and revenues than the online business alone.

The online business of Charles Schwab has similar characteristics, being a low-cost method of serving the firm's original core customers, most of whom wanted to use a sophisticated blend of both offline services (the branch network) and online trading. Many catalog companies such as L.L. Bean, J. Crew, and The Gap have found the same in extending their catalog business to a potentially superior economic model online. Indeed, analysis of the seventy-five most frequently visited Internet sites today shows more than three-quarters are clicks-and-mortar hybrids, where integration was more powerful than the turbocharge of a separate business with its own management and financial currency.

Redefinitions that change a highly strategic, core process and require integration into the core business are often best done internally. One example is Kodak's initiatives to shift to digital processing capabilities in its labs, with a range of new Internet services for processing digital images. Another is General Motors's bold and risky initiatives to allow consumers to custom order a new car online, reducing the elapsed order-to-delivery time from as long as eight weeks to a mere four to eleven days.

When the new business is strongly related to the core, but will never replace the original business, the best decision will rest on tactical trade-offs inherent in answers to the following:

- Is the new business better able to attract the talent it needs as an integrated entity or as an autonomous unit?

- Would the new business model receive a high valuation from the external stock market, and is such currency required to buy talent and invest in the business?

- Would separating the new business from the old foster the competition necessary to define customer boundaries where one model is superior to the other?

Based on its answers to these questions Staples.com, the online version of the office superstore Staples, chose to design and launch itself as a separate Internet business. Staples is one of the great business success stories of the past decade, being the fastest company ever to grow to $10 billion. But some customers find the traditional bricks-and-mortar offering less efficient than ordering office supplies online. In order to stake out this territory ahead of a variety of nascent online competitors, Staples set up Staples.com as a separate company in a physical location adjacent to the corporate headquarters. The start-up had about one hundred employees, whose mission was to sell an expanded version of the Staples product line over the Internet, with deliveries arranged from Staples's core distribution system. Staples.com was to be issued to the public as a tracking stock whose value was established in an initial round of funding by a 5 percent sale of the business to several venture capitalists. Founder Tom Stemberg and the Staples management team believed that this approach would attract talent and develop a separate Internet culture, thereby getting the company off to a quick start.

The Staples management team took several additional steps to balance the core with the need for independence. First, it established transfer prices for corporate services and products consistent with the costs to the retail stores and the wholesale channels. Second, it distributed stock options not only to the employees of the start-up, but to the employees in the parent company, all the way through to the retail store staff. Finally, it encouraged competition for the total customer base, discovering that the best accounts are those that buy through all channels and modes. We believe that more and more companies will opt for this hybrid business model, which balances the needs for independence and a separate currency to attract talent to the start-up with the needs for tight logistics and purchasing links with the core business.

Situation 2: Shifting Resources to a New Business Definition

Sometimes redefining the core entails making a change in the boundaries that define the business, requiring the establishment of a new entity that draws on skills and assets from the core but does not anticipate cannibalizing it extensively. There are three types of boundary changes: (1) the development of new intermediaries, such as exchanges, enabled by information technology; (2) the unbundling of the traditional value chain into its constituent activities; and (3) the radical and rapid broadening of customer product and service offerings enabled by a new technology.

New intermediaries that aggregate purchases, create a market, or provide a clearinghouse for industry information are proliferating. While many will not survive, some will prosper and reshape core business processes in many sectors. One example is the energy consortium Pantellos Corp., consisting of fifteen member-owners, including Consolidated Edison and First Energy Corp., recently formed to broker power flows and manage the supply chain in North America. Another example is the new entity initially called autoxchange, which was formed by Ford Motor Company and rapidly joined by other heavyweights such as General Motors and Daimler-Chrysler to aggregate purchasing power and to enable a paradigm shift to "build-to-order" methods. As a *Wall Street Journal* article observed:

> The unusual decision to collaborate puts the car compa-
> nies—leading examples of the old industrial economy—in
> the driver's seat of what could become the biggest business-
> to-business bazaar in the Internet-driven New Economy. It
> is intended to set a global standard for online purchasing in
> the auto industry and perhaps in other industries.[10]

In fact, auto-xchange is just one effort of Ford's ConsumerConnect business group, which is leading the e-business efforts across the company. Jacques Nasser, CEO of Ford Motor, "is on an Internet-economy learning curve. He's striking alliances throughout the high-tech world, seeking to transform Ford from what Wall Street regards as a metal-bending company into a more dynamic, Web-savvy consumer marketing firm." According to Nasser, "It means nothing less than the total reinvention of this company."[11] There is little in the automotive industry that would transform the core more than shifting to build-to-order, if it can really be accomplished.

Each of these new businesses, like dozens of others in industries ranging from airline parts to retail purchasing, will be spun off as separate entities to accommodate the structural need for separation and maximize neutrality. This is similar to the logic that guided the trailblazing creation of the Sabre system by American Airlines for industrywide reservations and flight data management, a system recently spun off to the public.

The second type of redefining a core business through making a radical shift in the business definition and boundaries is by unbundling the traditional value chain. The Internet allows for the cost-effective disintermediation of once-integrated chains of activities (such as a fully integrated distributor), in turn allowing new businesses to be developed around the outsourcing of particular activities or components that were formerly inefficient to separate. An example of this type of business is UPS e-Logistics. This new business has been set up separately, but within UPS, and it draws heavily on the infrastructure, information systems, customer relations, and experience base of UPS. Although not a true redefinition of the core, this initiative, if successful on a large scale, would have a significant and positive impact on UPS's prospects for sustainable growth.

New businesses that draw heavily on the core, but will not cannibalize the core to a great degree, are often best set up in separate units. Whether these units should be outside of the corporate structure and with outside ownership is primarily a function of three trade-offs:

1. Can the right talent be attracted inside, and is the existence or prospect of an initial public offering required to attract this talent?

2. Is separation required for strategic reasons, which generally stem from the need for neutrality or the need to avoid creating conflict with customers in the core business (such as competing with customers or with the channel)?

3. Would separation provide a source of public financing, because of high stock valuations, for making critical strategic acquisitions or investments?

Situation 3: Structural Redefinition of the Core

Economist Joseph Schumpeter, writing during the 1940s, argued that the earnings ability of any industrial concern diminishes over time. We would extend this observation to say that today, any core business that does not change fundamentally from time to time is bound to see its earnings capacity and its competitive position decline.

Sometimes redefining the core requires a rapid and massive redeployment of resources from the historic business to a promising adjacency. Earlier in the book, we noted that only about 3 percent of our sustained value creating companies were "shrinking value creators." Several of these companies made major structural changes to sell and replace their original core business, effectively reforming the company around a new core. PerkinElmer Instruments provides an example of a dramatic companywide redefinition of a core business from basic laboratory analytical instruments to instruments that analyze the sequencing of genes for biotechnology.

When Tony White took over Perkin-Elmer Corporation in 1995, the company was valued at $1.5 billion, and it consisted primarily of a wide range of niche-focused analytical instruments accumulated in the portfolio since its founding in 1932 by Richard Perkin and Charles Elmer. The original business, built on optical instrumentation, eventually extended from bombsights to satellite reconnaissance devices. The loose collection of businesses prompted some investors to suggest the company liquidate its product lines one by one to the highest bidder.

In the array of Perkin-Elmer's businesses, White noticed a small business that sold instruments that could perform high-speed genetic mapping and sequencing and was the apparent leader in its small, but promising niche. Over the next few years, the Perkin-Elmer team streamlined the original core businesses for sale to EG&G, a provider of management and technical services to governmental agencies, and shifted its investment resources to the gene-sequencing business, catching a research wave that carried biosystems revenues from $320 million to $1.2 billion in three years. White then split the company into PE Biosystems, the equipment manufacturer, and Celera Genomics, a sequencing business that buys and runs the sequencing equipment. Today, PE Biosystems (now called Applied Biosystems) and Celera are worth four times more than the original Perkin-Elmer that White inherited.

The genius of White and his management team was in recognizing the potential of the genetic-mapping business and in brilliantly redeploying and executing a complex strategy to shift the whole company's center of gravity. Beginning with a gem buried deep in the portfolio, they took advantage of a rapidly transforming market for biotechnology equipment and a remarkable product line hidden in their core business.

Sometimes redefinition by structural change takes longer, involving a much more extensive sequence of exits and capability acquisitions. Such a strategy comes with a high level of difficulty—and high failure rate. Still, there are some striking examples of success, few more so than Nokia.

Nokia began in 1865 as a mill for the manufacture of pulp and paper on the Nokia river in Finland. During the next 130 years, the company accumulated a range of regional industrial companies, creating a small conglomerate with businesses ranging from paper to electronics to rubber. In fact, rubber boots in Finland are still referred to as *nokia*. Nokia's transformation came from an inseparable combination of opportunism, smart decisions, and good fortune. In 1982, the company's leadership decided to work with the Finnish telecommunications industry to implement the first countrywide mobile phone system using the GSM standard. The first wireless phone call ever made was placed on this GSM system by the Finnish Prime Minister in 1991.

From then on, Nokia's leadership, especially its new CEO Jorma Ollila, saw the confluence of wireless technology and digital information as the place to begin betting the company. For the next few years, Ollila invested aggressively in plants to produce handsets and acquisitions to support the emerging telecommunications strategy. Nokia financed these investments by divesting many of its other businesses in rubber, cable, color TV, and energy. The cell phone story is still playing out technologically and competitively, but it fueled Nokia's growth from just $2 billion of revenues in 1993 to $19 billion in 1999, with margins that increased steadily. From almost nowhere, Nokia has captured 26.9 percent of the world cellular phone market, making it the clear leader. Granted, the company enjoyed good fortune in several respects: for instance, it invested in a cellular start-up at the right time, and GSM was a robust European standard in contrast to the balkanized North American systems. Nonetheless, Nokia remains a remarkable story of using acquisition to transform, indeed replace, an original core.

Other companies, such as Monsanto and Corning, also have relied on buying and selling to create a strong core. But more, including Xerox, Compaq, Sears, General Motors, Westinghouse, Zenith, and Olivetti, have fallen short. The approach takes time—and who is to say you will guess right? But there is a riskier approach still.

The most dramatic form of structural change to redefine a core business is the rarest of all—the complete shutdown of the original core business on an accelerated time scale and the movement to a totally new structure, possibly embedded within another existing company. Among Internet-driven transformations, relatively few companies have completely abandoned their offline business to transform into an exclusively Internet company. Most have adopted a hybrid mode. One that has made a complete transformation, out of desperation, is Egghead.

Egghead was founded in 1984 and became, along with Babbage's Etc., one of the first two leaders in software retailing. In 1992, Egghead was a familiar presence in suburban malls with 250 stores, 2,500 employees, and $700 million in sales. But the company was in trouble: it was heading toward permanent unprofitability in its stores and facing competition from superstores, catalogers, and soon the Internet. Over the next seven years, Egghead closed stores until 1998, when it decided to close its remaining stores and transform and move its business model online, naming itself Egghead.com. In 1999, the company furthered its transformation by merging with Onsale to create one of the largest online retailers. Though still unprofitable as the new model is refined online, Egghead epitomizes an extreme external transformation, creating a separate unit that eventually allowed the company to shut down its original core retail stores.

These are remarkable illustrations of rapid and dramatic shifts of a core business. In the case of PerkinElmer, the shift entailed selling the original core and redeploying resources into a relatively small product line at the periphery of the instrumentation business. For Nokia, the transformation extended over a longer period of time but was no less dramatic in its ultimate redeployment of a business opportunity embedded in one of several relatively stagnant core businesses. And for Egghead, the transformation was quick but still has to play out as the company encounters a new set of competitors, such as Amazon.com, in its new online arena.

In all of these cases, the transformation of the core resulted in new companies with a highly focused, new core business targeting leadership in a market with new definition and boundaries. Structural redefinitions of the core are not options that always, or even frequently, make sense. They require the confluence of several preconditions: the ideal core to migrate toward, a market growth environment where investors reward preemptive moves, a management team with a clear vision of a new future, and above all, the team's ability to execute highly difficult strategy.

Conclusion

Industry turbulence is hitting more rapidly and powerfully than most managers ever have seen. All of the data that we have calculated from our own efforts and found from outside sources supports the fact that decision times are shortening, uncertainty is increasing, and the range of fundamental strategic choices is widening. Many of the changes faced by executives require partial or complete rethinking of the fundamentals of their core business. In some cases, the required actions call for rapidly redefining part of the core, as the leaders of Dovebid did, or shifting resources to an entirely new core, as the leaders of PerkinElmer did. We have attempted to identify as many successful cases of companies redefining their core business as we could, yet have found many more instances of companies falling short. Redefinition is hard: most managers have never done it before, and it entails high risk. This is why the business community is experimenting with such a wide range of structural solutions.

The success cases cited suggest a few instructive caveats:

1. Do not redefine the core without a clear vision and set of strategic principles on which the management team agrees.

2. Do not redefine the core without first establishing a common point of view on how turbulence might play out and what positioning in the marketplace provides the greatest competitive advantage.

3. Explore the full range of structural options to balance the need for integration with the original core and the need for speed, which can be achieved with a separate entity.

4. Overinvest in management capacity and management processes at the start of a redefinition program.

5. Recognize the inherent uncertainty that has triggered the need to consider redefining a core business, which may require hedging strategies and diagnostics for constantly measuring the "strategic dashboard" and making midcourse corrections.

Most managers have quarterly earnings to deliver, core business cash flows to protect, employees in the original core who demand fair treatment, management team members with different points of view on the future, doubts of their own about the success of redefinition, and concerns about the complexity of execution. The low success rate of redefinition to date is rarely, in our experience, due to unskilled management; it is inherent in the complexity of the task. Even to attempt to redefine business fundamentals in a world where all systems act to protect and cling to the status quo calls for extraordinary leadership. It is here that we see most acutely our third paradox of growth: It is the management teams for which the cost of inaction is the greatest that often have the most difficulty embarking on a path to redefine their core. The true heroes of the Internet economy are those managers who try at all.

5

Growing from the Core

The research underlying this book on how companies grow shows clearly just how difficult it is to build, to maintain, and especially to transform a strong core business over a period of more than a few years. Some of the contributors to the thinking in this book are among the most talented and hardworking people we know. They have gathered around them extraordinary teams. Yet all have encountered downturns in the growth cycles of businesses in which they have been involved. So too, the greatest pilots have encountered turbulence, and the greatest coaches have had losing seasons. It is with this perspective that we regard our effort in this book. We do not suggest a formula for success—for there is none—but rather provide some strategic principles and self-diagnostic tools as references for even the most excellent managers of the strongest core businesses who must reconsider or reformulate their strategies. We believe that the principles described in this book can improve the odds of success but that no single set of ideas can guarantee it.

The research and writing of this book have been done over several years that overlap both the height of private equity investing and the dawn of and early returns from the Internet economy. Under all of these conditions, we have asked ourselves repeatedly whether the new ordering of leaders and followers might embody lessons that fundamentally change our thesis. Our conclusion: although we are witnessing a fundamental change in the way capital flows, valuations are made, and business is conducted, our central themes remain rock solid:

- Very few companies actually grow profitably and sustainably, though all plan to do so.

- Building unique strength in a core business, no matter how small or narrowly focused, is the key to subsequent growth. Many companies that neglect this principal retrench and return to the core.

- Most management teams underestimate the growth potential of their core and fail to mine all of its hidden value growth. In fact, the best core businesses are often the greatest underperformers relative to their true potential.

- Most successful companies achieve most of their growth by expanding into logical adjacencies that have shared economics and reinforce the core business, not from unrelated diversifications or moves into "hot" markets.

- Many of the most damaging mistakes in strategy derive from the tension between investing in the core and growing into adjacencies as well as in the specific choice of adjacencies.

- Industry turbulence often demands that the leader redefine his or her company's core business at a time when it appears at the height of its power.

- As simple as it sounds, achieving growth is hard because most organizations protect the status quo, and growth requires change.

These principles come as no surprise, but it is shocking to realize how often they are violated and how often they constitute the fulcrum of the most important issues of growth strategy.

Although these principles have not changed, their specific action implications in some sectors of the Internet economy have. Throughout our book, we have described contemporary adaptations of these principles, some of which are only now emerging or being debated. An example is the discussion about when to separate or integrate a new, possibly competitive business model.

Trigger Point for Shifting Emphasis

When is it appropriate to shift financial and management resources from the core business to surrounding adjacencies? Even more difficult, what are the warning signs that signal the need to shift a fundamental element in the core business? The constant tension between mining the core and breaking out into something new exists in every business. The way the management team deals with this tension is a key determinant of the prospects for future sustained, profitable growth.

Figure 5-1 is based on our data on more than eighty-two hundred companies that is used throughout this book to study the incidence of profitable growth worldwide. The figure shows the total ten-year return to shareholders from various combinations of growth in earnings and growth in revenue. Obviously, companies that grow neither earnings nor revenue at more than 5 percent earn modest returns, averaging 6.9 percent. Companies that achieve growth over 15 percent in earnings and revenue benefit from a multiplier effect, earning ten-year shareholder returns of 25.8 percent.

But particularly interesting, from the point of view of our discussion of tension between core focus and adjacency growth, are the companies represented by the two other cells in the figure. Companies that allow their revenue growth to drift to 5 percent or below while they focus on mining the core for cost reduction and asset turns receive relatively low rewards from the public markets. Indeed, a ten-year record of 15 percent or more earnings growth in a company with low revenue growth will yield a shareholder return of only 9.5 percent on average. This is the challenge many large core businesses face in setting budgets and earnings targets; it is usually easier year after year to mine the core for twelve more months. Yet, at some point, margin expansion potential ends. Then what?

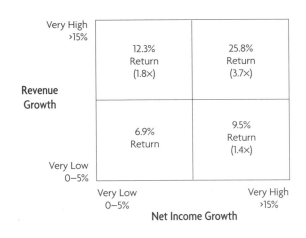

5-1 Sustained Value Creators Achieve the Highest Returns

Source: Worldscope database; Bain analysis.

Note: All growth rates are real. Number of companies = 932 (companies from 1,854-company database with both net income compound annual growth rate and revenue compound annual growth rate over the ten-year period 1988–1998 of > 0). Annual total shareholder return is calculated as compound annual total shareholder return over the ten-year period 1988–1998.

Finally, consider companies that expand into adjacencies aggressively—possibly too aggressively—diluting the quality of their earnings and creating larger but less profitable companies. These companies grew revenues over ten years by over 15 percent but achieved earnings growth of less than 5 percent, seeing their margins steadily decline due to their movement into new business areas in which they had less expertise and that offered less profitability. Literally thousands of companies follow this pattern. The stories of some, such as Compaq Computer, Bausch & Lomb, and Saatchi & Saatchi, are told in this book. Again, an unbalanced approach to growth leads to investor skepticism about the future and low valuations.

Our multiyear growth study leads us to several questions managers should ask as they reflect on their own strategies:

- What is our primary focus now (optimizing the core, adjacencies, redefinition)? Many managers, we find, are not sure.

- How many of our resources are focused on areas that have the potential to build market power and influence and drive for segment leadership? How many are focused on inevitable follower positions?

- Where has our growth come from in the past two years, and what is the plan for the next three years? Where have recent plans fallen short or exceeded expectations?
  - share gain in the core
  - shift in the business mix to growing segments and channels
  - pricing
  - new core products
  - cost reduction
  - new customers or share gain in existing customers
  - adjacencies involving new customers or new products

- Are we experiencing unusual levels (high or low) of attrition of the most progressive managers or customers? Where are they going, or where are they coming from?

- Where are our competitors focused in terms of the core, adjacencies, and redefinition?

- Are unconventional competitors making incursions at the fringe of our business?

Armed with this data, and ideas and examples like those in this book, managers should be constantly vigilant in tracking the three most dangerous long-term patterns we have identified. The first is premature abandonment of the core in favor of far-flung new adjacencies. Signs of erosion in the core or diffusion across too many initiatives will reveal this problem. The second is excessive mining of a core business, failing to put in place large enough new growth vehicles soon enough. If more earnings growth is consistently coming from these operating and cost-based initiatives than from core growth, there is clear danger. The third pattern is failure to anticipate the need for core redefinition. By the time competitors with new business models are taking your customers, you have probably waited too long to react.

Is It an Organizational Problem or a Strategy Problem?

A key issue for senior executives wrestling with growth problems or frustrations is determining whether the company's strategy is wrong or whether the organization is not able to execute it. Sometimes these problems can coexist and are difficult to separate. A strategy built for an organization that cannot execute it is not a good strategy, by definition. Conversely, a superb organization can shape and adapt even a mediocre strategy into a winner.

In high-growth markets, the most common organization-versus-strategy problem is inadequate management capacity for growth and rapid decision making combined with a lack of central direction, allowing many marginal and defocusing growth initiatives to sap resources. Jim Vincent, CEO of Biogen, a classic "profit from the core" success story, has argued convincingly in interviews that this capacity issue is the number one CEO growth constraint, in his experience. The solution involves focusing more tightly around a strategy and, frequently, introducing management capabilities to deal with a larger, more complex, faster-moving company. The history of management in both the computer industry and Internet start-ups shows this pattern over and over.

In lower-growth markets, the most common problem is excessive mining of the core combined with a failure to see the emerging new landscape and possibilities. Often the historic management team has done a superb job of building and tending the core but along the way has acquired biases and habits that make it difficult to see the need for and commit serious resources to a strategic shift. The solution often requires the injection of new management talent along with a strategic redirection.

Ten Key Questions for Management

We close with ten questions that we believe management teams should periodically ask themselves about their companies and should include at the start of every review of their basic growth strategy. Certainly, companies find themselves in an almost infinite variety of strategic situations. However, we believe that these questions have universal applicability for companies ranging from dominant product businesses trying to decide how to deal with the Internet to distribution companies wrestling with the sudden unbundling of their value chain to online companies trying to look beyond the "profitless prosperity" dream of today toward the requirements for sustained, profitable growth.

1. What is the most tightly defined profitable core of our business, and is it gaining or losing strength?

2. What defines the boundaries of the business that we are competing for, and where are those boundaries going to shift in the future?

3. Are there new competitors currently at the fringe of our business that pose potential longer-term threats to the core?

4. Are we certain that we are achieving the full strategic and operating potential of our core business, the "hidden value" of the core?

5. What is the full set of potential adjacencies to our core business and possible adjacency moves (single or multiple moves)? Are we looking at these in a planned, logical sequence or piecemeal?

6. What is our point of view on the future of the industry? As a team, do we have consensus? How is this point of view shaping our adjacency strategy and point of arrival?

7. Should major new growth initiatives be pursued inside, next to, or outside the core? How should we decide?

8. Is industry turbulence changing the fundamental source of future competitive advantage? How? Through new models? New

segments? New competitors? And what are we monitoring on a regular basis?

9. Are organizational enablers and inhibitors to growth in the right balance for the needed change?

10. What are the guiding strategic principles that should apply consistently to all of our major strategic and operating decisions?

Although military analogies to strategy are currently out of favor, we remain struck by the contemporary relevance of this observation from Sun-Tzu's *Art of War:* "The more opportunities that I seize, the more opportunities that multiply before me."[1] This phenomenon is at the heart of growth strategy and embodies the fundamental tension between protecting the core and driving into more and more adjacencies, propelled by greater and greater success. The Alexander problem described earlier will always be with us. However, we hope that the guiding principles and lessons learned from success and failure can help improve the odds for business managers battling in a world of greater uncertainty, more options, less time, bigger rewards and penalties, and higher complexity than ever before.

Notes

Chapter 1: Desperately Seeking Growth

1. Charles Goldsmith, "A Dying Lens Maker Zooms Back," *Wall Street Journal*, 23 March 2000.
2. John Micklethwait and Adrian Wooldridge, "Oxford Dons vs. Management Gurus," *Wall Street Journal*, 8 November 1996.
3. In a sense, our definition is a long-term version of the definitions used by G. Bennett Stewart III in *The Quest for Value*, which drive off of economic returns relative to the long-term cost of capital.
4. Bernard Wysocki, Jr., "Corporate America Confronts the Meaning of a 'Core' Business," *Wall Street Journal*, 9 November 1999.
5. Clayton M. Christensen, *The Innovator's Dilemma: When New Technologies Cause Great Firms to Fail* (Boston: Harvard Business School Press, 1997).
6. Carl Shapiro and Hal R. Varian, *Information Rules: A Strategic Guide to the Network Economy* (Boston: Harvard Business School Press, 1999).

Chapter 2: The Profitable Core

1. Mitt Romney, interview by Chris Zook, Boston, 12 June 1998.
2. David Sadtler, Andrew Campbell, and Richard Koch, *Break Up!* (Oxford: Capstone Publishing, 1997), 33.
3. Andrew Bary, "Why Catch a Knife?" *Barron's*, 6 October 1997, 17.
4. Steven Lipin and Nikhil Deogun, "Pepsi Announces Spinoff of Eateries, and Stock Soars," *Wall Street Journal*, 24 January 1997.
5. Ibid.

6. Steven Lipin and Nikhil Deogun, "Pepsi Shares Leap on Report of Spinoff of Restaurant Unit," *Wall Street Journal Europe,* 24 January 1997.

7. Constantinos C. Markides, *Diversification, Refocusing, and Economic Performance* (Cambridge: MIT Press, 1995), 9.

8. Michael E. Porter, "From Competitive Advantage to Corporate Strategy," *Harvard Business Review,* May–June 1987.

9. Michael Dell, interview by Chris Zook, Dell headquarters, Austin, TX, 26 March 1999. See also Michael Dell with Catherine Fredman, *Direct from Dell: Strategies That Revolutionized an Industry* (New York: HarperBusiness, 1999).

10. Philip Evans and Thomas S. Wurster, *Blown to Bits: How the New Economics of Information Transforms Strategy* (Boston: Harvard Business School Press, 1999) and "Getting Real About Virtual Commerce," *Harvard Business Review,* November–December 1999. By far the best integrated and most original view on this topic is Carl Shapiro and Hal R. Varian, *Information Rules: A Strategic Guide to the Network Economy* (Boston: Harvard Business School Press, 1999). For additional readings on topics that bear on the increased blurring of business definition and the management challenges in the Internet economy, see Joan Magretta, ed., *Managing in the New Economy* (Boston: Harvard Business School Press, 1999).

    Until the late 1970s, most business definition was put in terms of products and traditional market boundaries. In the 1980s, writers and theorists such as Derek Abell began looking more fundamentally at boundaries created by basic customer need (e.g., transportation versus railroad) and technology as potential ways to define a business. The next wave of thinking (Prahalad and Hamel) introduced the idea of the core competence as a source of ultimate competitive advantage in a core business and as a way of defining the boundaries of a businesses. For instance, recognizing Service-Master's expertise at managing large numbers of employees performing basic services leads to a clearer understanding of its business definition than looking just at cleaning services for businesses.

11. Frederick F. Reichheld. *The Loyalty Effect: The Hidden Force Behind Growth, Profits, and Lasting Value* (Boston: Harvard Business School Press, 1996).

12. Bain & Company, "The Value of Online Customer Loyalty and How You Can Capture It," monograph, Bain & Company, Boston, 2000.

13. A recent study of prototyping illustrates this: "When Sony president Nobuyuki Idei casually remarks that the consumer electronics giant typically takes about a week to progress from a new product concept to a rough working prototype, the comment says less about Sony's technological prowess than about its predisposition toward rapid design." (Michael

Schrage, *Serious Play: How the World's Best Companies Simulate to Innovate* [Boston: Harvard Business School Press, 2000], 63.) This predisposition is at the center of Sony's profitable core. The company epitomizes both the fast follower in existing markets (television, game stations, laptop VAIO computer) and the ability to develop new-to-world products (Walkman, MP3 recorder with memory stick).

14. Carl Everett, interview by Chris Zook, Austin, TX, 17 February 1999.
15. Paul Larson, "Advanced Micro Devices, Inc.: How Did It Find Trouble?" 5 March 1999, <www.fool.com> (15 November 1999).
16. For the best statement of this general point of view, see Michael Porter, "What Is Strategy?" *Harvard Business Review*, November–December 1996.

Chapter 3: The Alexander Problem

1. Allan Sloan, "80's Deals Showed American Express Could Use a Dose of Street Smarts," *Washington Post*, 16 March 1993.
2. Alex Pham, "Microsoft Targets America's Gamers," *Boston Globe*, 11 March 2000.
3. David Sheff, "Sony's Plan for World Recreation," *Wired*, November 1999, 3.
4. Gretchen Morgenson, "On the Acquisitions Road, Stay Alert to the Hazards," *Sunday New York Times*, 10 October 1999, sec. 3, p. 1.
5. Ibid.
6. Chris Reidyo, "Gillette Sells Its Stationery Line," *Boston Globe*, 23 August 2000.
7. James C. Collins and Jerry I. Porras, *Built to Last: Successful Habits of Visionary Companies* (New York: HarperBusiness, 1994), 141.
8. Jay McCormack, "Amazing Grace: ServiceMaster Industries, Inc.," *Forbes*, 17 June 1985, 83.
9. Ron Grover, *The Disney Touch: Disney, ABC & the Quest for the World's Greatest Media Empire* (Chicago: Irwin Professional Publishing), 3.
10. Bruce Orwall and Matthew Rose, "Disney Held Talks with Conde Nast, Hearst to Sell Fairchild Magazine Unit," *Wall Street Journal*, 16 August 1999.
11. Phil Buxton, "New Medicine," *Marketing Week*, 26 October 1999, 28.
12. Donald Read, *The Power of News: The History of Reuters*, 2d ed. (London, Oxford University Press, 1999), 12.
13. C. K. Prahalad and Gary Hamel, "Core Competence of the Corporation," *Harvard Business Review*, May–June 1990, 79.
14. Perhaps the best survey of this topic is provided by Carl Shapiro and Hal Varian in *Information Rules: A Strategic Guide to the Network Economy* (Boston: Harvard Business School Press, 1999).

15. We do not address this topic in this book; however, see Martha Amram and Nalin Kulatilaka, *Real Options: Managing Strategic Investment in an Uncertain World* (Boston: Harvard Business School Press, 1999).

16. R. Scott Raynovich, "Intel's Got Internet Inside," *Redherring.com,* 11 August 1999.

17. Ibid.

18. John Keegan, *The Mask of Command* (New York: Viking–Elisabeth Sifton Books, 1987), 83–84.

19. Mitt Romney, interview by Chris Zook, Boston, 12 June 1998.

20. Orit Gadiesh and James L. Gilbert, "Profit Pools: A Fresh Look at Strategy," *Harvard Business Review,* May–June 1998, 141.

Chapter 4: The Redefinition Dilemma

1. Throughout this book, we have used analogies from biology. More than any other source, we have drawn our understanding, as well as this example, from Edward O. Wilson, *The Diversity of Life* (Cambridge: Belknap Press of Harvard University Press, 1992).

2. In the future, sustained growth companies will be those that have been able to respond to today's turbulence in their industry and use it as a catalyst for change. A recent Bain survey of senior executives suggested that 91 percent of them believed that industry turbulence makes having a clear strategy more important than ever. Over 61 percent of them stated that they were worried about turbulence, and 73 percent said that they felt that their organizations suffered a false sense of security. (Darrell Rigby, "Winning in Turbulence," Bain & Company, Boston, 1999.) Those companies whose core businesses may need fundamental redefinition will face the difficult choice of transforming internally or developing a separate business into which skills and assets from the original core business are infused.

3. W. Chan Kim and Renee Mauborgne, "Strategy, Value Innovation and the Knowledge Economy," *Sloan Management Review,* Spring 1999.

4. Arie de Geus, "The Living Company," *Harvard Business Review,* March–April 1997, 23.

5. "How to Live Long and Prosper," *Economist,* 10 May 1997.

6. There is a massive body of literature about the remarkably poor record of results that came from the reengineering fad. See the following: John P. Kotter, "Leading Change: Why Transformational Efforts Fail," *Harvard Business Review,* March–April 1995; Fran Simons, "Transforming Change," *Australian Financial Review,* 26 March 1999; Constant D. Beugre, "Implementing Business Process Reengineering," *Journal of Applied Behavioral Science,* 34, no. 3 (1998); Thomas A. Stewart, "Reengineering: The Hot New

Managing Tool," *Fortune,* 23 August 1993; and Brian Harrison, "How to Fail at Reengineering," *Directors & Boards,* Fall 1994.

7. Gary Jacobson and John Hillkirk, *Xerox: American Samurai* (New York: Collier Books, 1986).

8. Kerry A. Dolan, "Judo Attack," *Forbes,* 9 March 1998, 62.

9. Rajesh K. Chandy and Gerald J. Tellis, "Organizing for Radical Product Innovation: The Overlooked Role of Willingness to Cannibalize," *Journal of Marketing Research,* November 1998.

10. Robert L. Simison, Fara Warner, and Gregory L. White, "Big Three Car Makers Plan Net Exchange—GM, Ford, DaimlerChrysler to Create a Single Firm to Supply Auto Parts," *Wall Street Journal,* 28 February 2000.

11. William J. Holstein, "The Dot Com within Ford," *U.S. News & World Report,* 7 February 2000, 34.

Chapter 5: Growing from the Core

1. Sun-Tzu, *The Art of War* (London: Oxford University Press, 1984).

Bibliography

Books

Abell, Derek. *Defining the Business: The Starting Point of Strategic Planning.* New York: Prentice-Hall, 1980.

Amram, Martha, and Nalin Kulatilaka. *Real Options: Managing Strategic Investment in an Uncertain World.* Boston: Harvard Business School Press, 1999.

Burrough, Bryan. *Barbarians at the Gate: The Fall of RJR Nabisco.* New York: HarperCollins, 1991.

Chandler, Alfred D., Jr. *Scale and Scope: The Dynamics of Industrial Capitalism.* Cambridge: The Belknap Press of Harvard University Press, 1990.

Christensen, Clayton M. *The Innovator's Dilemma: When New Technologies Cause Great Firms to Fail.* Boston: Harvard Business School Press, 1997.

Cody, Thomas G. *Innovating for Health: The Story of Baxter International.* Deerfield, IL: Baxter International Inc., 1994.

Collins, Douglas. *America's Favorite Food: The Story of Campbell Soup Company.* New York: Harry N. Adams, 1994.

Collins, James C., and Jerry I. Porras. *Built to Last: Successful Habits of Visionary Companies.* New York: HarperBusiness, 1997.

Davies, S., et. al. *The Dynamics of Market Leadership in the U.K. Manufacturing Industry 1979–1986.* London: Centre for Business Strategy, 1991.

Day, George S., and David J. Reibstein. *Wharton on Dynamic Competitive Strategy.* New York: John Wiley & Sons, 1997.

De Geus, Arie. *The Living Company.* Boston: Harvard Business School Press, 1997.

Dell, Michael, with Catherine Fredman. *Direct from Dell: Strategies That Revolutionized an Industry.* New York: HarperBusiness, 1999.

Evans, Philip, and Thomas S. Wurster. *Blown to Bits: How the New Economics of Information Transforms Strategy.* Boston: Harvard Business School Press, 1999.

Farkas, Charles M., Philippe De Backer, and Allen Sheppard. *Maximum Leadership: The World's Top Leaders Discuss How They Add Value to Companies.* London: Orion, 1995.

Goold, Michael, Andrew Campbell, and Marcus Alexander. *Corporate-Level Strategy: Creating Value in the Multibusiness Company.* New York: John Wiley & Sons, 1994.

Grove, Andrew S. *Only the Paranoid Survive: How to Exploit the Crisis Points That Challenge Every Company.* New York: Bantam Books, 1999.

Grover, Ron. *The Disney Touch: Disney, ABC & the Quest for the World's Greatest Media Empire.* Chicago: Irwin Professional Publishing.

Hamel, Gary. *Leading the Revolution.* Boston: Harvard Business School Press, 2000.

Hamel, Gary, and C. K. Prahalad. *Competing for the Future.* Boston: Harvard Business School Press, 1994.

Hannan, Michael T., and John Freeman. *Organizational Ecology.* Cambridge: Harvard University Press, 1989.

Harvard Business Review on Strategies for Growth. Boston: Harvard Business School Press, 1998.

Imparato, Nicholas, and Oren Harari. *Jumping the Curve.* San Francisco: Jossey-Bass Publishers, 1994.

Jackson, Tim. *Inside Intel.* New York: Penguin Books, 1997.

Jacobson, Gary, and John Hillkirk. *Xerox: American Samurai.* New York: Collier Books, Macmillan Publishing, 1986.

Janus, Irving. *Groupthink.* Boston: Houghton Mifflin, 1982.

Jonash, Ronald S., and Tom Sommerlatte. *The Innovation Premium.* New York: Perseus Books, 1999.

Kaplan, Robert S., and David P. Norton. *The Balanced Scorecard: Translating Strategy into Action.* Boston: Harvard Business School Press, 1996.

Katz, Donald. *Just Do It.* Holbrook, MA: Adams Media Corp., 1997.

Keegan, John. *The Mask of Command.* New York: Viking–Elisabeth Sifton Books, 1987.

Keynes, John Maynard. *A Treatise on Probability.* London: Macmillan, 1921.

Leonard-Barton, Dorothy. *Wellsprings of Knowledge.* Cambridge: Harvard Business School Press, 1995.

Magretta, Joan, ed. *Managing in the New Economy.* Boston: Harvard Business School Press, 1999.

Markides, Constantinos C. *Diversification, Refocusing, and Economic Performance.* Cambridge: MIT Press, 1995.

Mintzberg, Henry. *The Rise and Fall of Strategic Planning.* New York: Prentice-Hall, 1994.

Montgomery, Cynthia A., and Michael E. Porter, eds. *Strategy: Seeking and Securing Competitive Advantage.* Boston: Harvard Business School Press, 1991.

Moore, Geoffrey A. *Inside the Tornado: Marketing Strategies from Silicon Valley's Cutting Edge.* New York: HarperBusiness, 1995.

———. *Crossing the Chasm: Marketing and Selling High-Tech Products to Mainstream Consumers.* New York: HarperBusiness, 1999.

Peters, Thomas J., and Robert H. Waterman, Jr. *In Search of Excellence: Lessons from America's Best-Run Companies.* New York: Harper & Row Publishers, 1982.

Porter, Michael E. *Competitive Strategy.* New York: Free Press, 1980.

———. *Competitive Advantage.* New York: Free Press, 1985.

Pottruck, David S., and Terry Pearce. *Clicks and Mortar: Passion-Driven Growth in an Internet-Driven World.* San Francisco: Jossey-Bass Publishers, 2000.

Quinn, James Brian, Jordan J. Baruch, and Karen Anne Zien. *Innovation Explosion: Using Intellect and Software to Revolutionize Growth Strategies.* New York: Free Press, 1997.

Ravenscroft, David J., Robert D. Buzzell, and Bradley T. Gale. *The PIMS Principles: Linking Strategy to Performance.* New York: Free Press, 1987.

Read, Donald. *The Power of News: The History of Reuters,* 2d ed. Oxford: Oxford University Press, 1999.

Reichheld, Frederick F. *The Loyalty Effect: The Hidden Force Behind Growth, Profits, and Lasting Value.* Boston: Harvard Business School Press, 1996.

Rothschild, Michael. *Bionomics: Economy as Ecosystem.* New York: Henry Holt, 1990.

Rumelt, Richard P., Dan E. Schendel, and David J. Teece, eds. *Fundamental Issues in Strategy: A Research Agenda.* Boston: Harvard Business School Press, 1994.

Sadtler, David, Andrew Campbell, and Richard Koch. *Break Up!* Oxford: Capstone Publishing, 1997.

Schrage, Michael. *Serious Play: How the World's Best Companies Simulate to Innovate.* Cambridge: Harvard Business School Press, 2000.

Schumpeter, Joseph. *Capitalism, Socialism and Democracy.* New York: Harper, 1942.

Shapiro, Carl, and Hal R. Varian. *Information Rules: A Strategic Guide to the Network Economy.* Boston: Harvard Business School Press, 1999.

Shiller, Robert. *Irrational Exuberance.* Princeton: Princeton University Press, 2000.

Sirower, Mark L. *The Synergy Trap: How Companies Lose the Acquisition Game.* New York: Free Press, 1997.

Slater, Robert. *Jack Welch and the GE Way.* New York: McGraw-Hill, 1999.

Slywotzky, Adrian J. *Value Migration: How to Think Several Moves Ahead of the Competition.* Boston: Harvard Business School Press, 1995.

Stalk, George Jr., and Thomas M. Hout. *Competing Against Time: How Time-Based Competition is Reshaping Global Markets.* New York: Free Press, 1990.

Stemberg, Thomas S. *Staples for Success.* Santa Monica, CA: Knowledge Exchange, 1996.

Stewart, G. Bennett III. *The Quest for Value.* New York: Stern/Stewart, 1993.

Sun-Tzu. *The Art of War.* London: Oxford University Press, 1984.

Swisher, Kara. *aol.com.* New York: Random House, 1998.

Tichy, Noel M., and Stratford Sherman. *Control Your Destiny or Someone Else Will.* London: HarperCollins, 1995.

Utterback, James M. *Mastering the Dynamics of Innovation.* Boston: Harvard Business School Press, 1994.

Wilson, Edward O. *The Diversity of Life.* Cambridge: Harvard University Press, 1992.

Articles

Abell, Derek F. "Competing Today While Preparing for Tomorrow." *Sloan Management Review,* Spring 1999.

Anslinger, and Thomas E. Copeland. "Growth Through Acquisitions: A Fresh Look." *Harvard Business Review,* January–February 1996.

Avila, Joe, Nat Mass, and Mark Turchan. "Keys to Profitable Growth." *The McKinsey Quarterly,* no. 1 (1996).

Baden-Fuller, Charles and Henk W. Volberda. "Strategic Renewal: How Large Complex Organizations Prepare for the Future." *International Studies of Management & Organization,* 22 June 1997.

Bain & Company. "The Value of Online Customer Loyalty and How You Can Capture It." *Monograph,* Bain & Company, Boston, 2000.

Bary, Andrew. "Why Catch a Knife?" *Barron's,* 6 October 1997.

Bechek, Bob, and Chris Zook. "The Jenga Phenomenon." White paper, Bain & Company, Boston, 1999.

Beinhocker, Eric D. "Robust Adaptive Strategies." *Sloan Management Review,* Spring 1999.

Berger, Philip, and Eli Ofek. "Diversification's Effect on Firm Value." *Journal of Financial Economics,* 37 (1995).

Beugre, Constant D. "Implementing Business Process Reengineering." *Journal of Applied Behavioral Science,* 34, no. 3 (1998).

Bower, Joseph L., and Clayton M. Christensen. "Disruptive Technologies: Catching the Wave." *Harvard Business Review,* January–February 1995.

Brian, W. Arthur. "Increasing Returns and the New World of Business." *Harvard Business Review,* July–August 1996.

Brooks, Rick. "UPS's New eVentures Unit Plans to Expand Logistics Business." *Wall Street Journal,* 7 February 2000.

Buxton, Phil. "New Medicine." *Marketing Week,* 26 October 1999.

Campbell, Andrew, Michael Goold, and Marcus Alexander. "Corporate Strategy: The Quest for Parenting Advantage." *Harvard Business Review,* March–April 1995.

Caves, Richard E., B. T. Gale, and Michael E. Porter. "Interfirm Profitability Differences." *Quarterly Journal of Economics,* November 1977.

Chandy, Rajesh K., and Gerald J. Tellis. "Organizing for Radical Product Innovation: The Overlooked Role of Willingness to Cannibalize." *Journal of Marketing Research,* November 1998.

Charan, Ram, and Geoffrey Colvin. "Why CEOs Fail." *Fortune,* 21 June 1999.

Collis, David J., and Cynthia A. Montgomery. "Competing on Resources: Strategy in the 1990s." *Harvard Business Review,* July–August 1995.

Comment, Robert, and Gregg A. Jarrell. "Corporate Focus and Stock Returns." *Journal of Financial Economics,* 37 (1995).

Corporate Strategy Board. "Stall Points: Barriers to Growth for the Large Corporate Enterprise." Monograph, The Advisory Board Company, Washington, DC, 1997.

Courtney, Hugh, Jane Kirkland, and Patrick Viguerie. "Strategy Under Uncertainty." *Harvard Business Review,* November–December 1997.

D'Aveni, Richard A. "Strategic Supremacy through Disruption and Dominance." *Sloan Management Review,* Spring 1999.

Day, George S. "Creating a Market Driven Organization." *Sloan Management Review,* Fall 1999.

de Geus, Arie. "The Living Company." *Harvard Business Review,* March–April 1997.

DeLlosa, Patty. "How Coke Is Kicking Pepsi's Can." *Fortune,* 28 October 1996.

Dolan, Kerry A. "Judo Attack." *Forbes,* 9 March 1998.

Drucker, Peter F. "The Information Executives Truly Need." *Harvard Business Review,* January–February 1995.

Eisenhardt, Kathleen M., and Shona L. Brown. "The Art of Continuous Change: Linking Complexity Theory and Time-Paced Evolution in Relentlessly Shifting Organizations." *Administrative Science Quarterly,* March 1997.

———. "Time Pacing: Competing in Markets That Won't Stand Still." *Harvard Business Review,* March–April 1998.

———. "Patching: Restitching Business Portfolios in Dynamic Markets." *Harvard Business Review,* May–June 1999.

Evans, Philip B. and Thomas S. Wurster. "Strategy and the New Economics of Information." *Harvard Business Review,* September–October 1997.

———. "Getting Real About Virtual Commerce." *Harvard Business Review,* November–December 1999.

Farkas, Charles M., and Bob Bechek. "Rebuilding Banking Piecemeal, On Web." *American Banker,* 28 May 1999.

Farkas, Charles M., and Suzy Wetlaufer. "The Ways Chief Executive Officers Lead." *Harvard Business Review,* May–June 1996.

"Fear of the Unknown." *Economist,* 4 December 1999.

Finnie, William C. "A Four-Cycle Approach to Strategy Development and Implementation." *Strategy & Leadership,* January–February 1997.

Fisher, Anne B. "Making Change Stick." *Fortune,* 17 April 1995.

"Fortune 500." *Fortune,* 26 April 1999.

Gadiesh, Orit, and James L. Gilbert. "How to Map Your Industry's Profit Pool." *Harvard Business Review,* May–June 1998.

———. "Profit Pools: A Fresh Look at Strategy." *Harvard Business Review,* May–June 1998.

Geroski, Paul A. "Early Warning of New Rivals." *Sloan Management Review,* Spring 1999.

Goldsmith, Charles. "A Dying Lens Maker Zooms Back." *Wall Street Journal,* 23 March 2000.

Goold, Michael and Andrew Campbell. "Many Best Ways to Make Strategy." *Harvard Business Review,* November–December 1987.

———. "Desperately Seeking Synergy." *Harvard Business Review,* September–October 1998.

Hamel, Gary. "Strategy as Revolution." *Harvard Business Review,* July–August 1996.

———. "Killer Strategies That Make Shareholders Rich." *Fortune,* 23 June 1997.

———. "Opinion: Strategy Innovation and the Quest for Value." *Sloan Management Review,* Winter 1998.

Hamel, Gary, and C. K. Prahalad. "Competing for the Future." *Harvard Business Review,* July–August 1994.

Hannan, Michael T., and John Freeman. "Structural Inertia and Organizational Change." *American Sociological Review,* April 1984.

Harrison, Brian. "How to Fail at Reengineering." *Directors & Boards,* Fall 1994.

Hart, Stuart L., and Mark B. Milstein. "Global Sustainability and the Creative Destruction of Industries." *Sloan Management Review,* Fall 1999.

Henderson, Bruce D. "The Origins of Strategy." *Harvard Business Review,* November–December 1989.

Holstein, William J. "The Dot Com within Ford." *U.S. News & World Report,* 7 February 2000.

"How to Live Long and Prosper." *Economist,* 10 May 1997.

Kaplan, Robert S., and David P. Norton. "The Balanced Scorecard: Measures That Drive Performance." *Harvard Business Review,* January–February 1992.

Kim, W. Chan, and Renee Mauborgne. "Value Innovation: The Strategic Logic of High Growth." *Harvard Business Review,* January–February 1997.

———. "When Competitive Advantage Is Neither." *Wall Street Journal,* Managers Journal, 21 April 1997.

———. "Strategy, Value Innovation and the Knowledge Economy." *Sloan Management Review,* Spring 1999.

Knight, Charles F. "Emerson Electric: Consistent Profits, Consistently." *Harvard Business Review,* January–February 1992.

Kotter, John P. "Leading Change: Why Transformational Efforts Fail." *Harvard Business Review,* March–April 1995.

Larson, Paul. "Advanced Micro Devices, Inc.: How Did It Find Trouble?" 5 March 1999. <www.fool.com> (15 November 1999).

Leonard, Russell L., Jr. "Reengineering: The Missing Links." *Human Resource Planning,* 19, no. 4 (1996).

Leonard-Barton, Dorothy. "Core Capabilities and Core Rigidities: A Paradox in Managing New Product Development." *Strategic Management Journal,* 13 (1992).

Lipin, Steven, and Nikhil Deogun. "Pepsi Announces Spinoff of Eateries, and Stock Soars." *Wall Street Journal,* 24 January 1997.

———. "Pepsi Shares Leap on Report of Spinoff of Restaurant Unit." *Wall Street Journal Europe,* 24 January 1997.

Markides, Constantinos C. "Strategic Innovation." *Sloan Management Review,* Spring 1997.

———. "To Diversify or Not To Diversify." *Harvard Business Review,* November–December 1997.

———. "Strategic Innovation in Established Companies." *Sloan Management Review,* Spring 1998.

———. "A Dynamic View of Strategy." *Sloan Management Review,* Spring 1999.

Marshall, Cheri T., and Robert D. Buzzell. "PIMS and the FTC Line-Of-Business Data: A Comparison." *Strategic Management Journal,* 11 (1990).

McCormack, Jay. "Amazing Grace: ServiceMaster Industries, Inc." *Forbes,* 17 June 1985.

Micklethwait, John, and Adrian Wooldridge. "Oxford Dons vs. Management Gurus." *Wall Street Journal,* 8 November 1996.

Mintzberg, Henry, and Joseph Lampel. "Reflecting on the Strategy Process." *Sloan Management Review,* Spring 1999.

Monk, Nina. "Title Fight." *Fortune,* 21 June 1999.

Morgenson, Gretchen. "On the Acquisitions Road, Stay Alert to the Hazards." *Sunday New York Times,* 10 October 1999.

O'Reilly, Brian. "They've Got Mail: UPS vs. FedEx." *Fortune,* 7 February 2000.

Orwall, Bruce, and Matthew Rose. "Disney Held Talks with Conde Nast, Hearst to Sell Fairchild Magazine Unit." *Wall Street Journal,* 16 August 1999.

Pham, Alex. "Microsoft Targets America's Gamers." *Boston Globe,* 11 March 2000.

Porter, Michael E. "From Competitive Advantage to Corporate Strategy." *Harvard Business Review,* May–June 1987.

———. "What Is Strategy?" *Harvard Business Review,* November–December 1996.

Prahalad, C. K., and Gary Hamel. "Core Competence of the Corporation." *Harvard Business Review,* May–June 1990.

Prahalad, C. K., and Venkatram Ramaswamy. "Co-opting Customer Competence." *Harvard Business Review,* January–February 2000.

Quinn, Sue. "Nokia Share Price Stays Upwardly Mobile." *Sun Herald,* 23 January 2000.

Raynovich, R. Scott. "Intel's Got Internet Inside." *Redherring.com,* 11 August 1999.

Reidyo, Chris. "Gillette Sells Its Stationery Line." *Boston Globe,* 23 August 2000.

Reingold, Jennifer. "Doesn't Work, Doesn't Matter." *Business Week,* 31 May 1999.

Rigby, Darrell K. "What's Today's Special At the Consultants' Café?" *Fortune,* 7 September 1998.

———. "Management Tools & Techniques 1999: An Executive's Guide." Bain & Company, Boston, 1999.

———. "Winning in Turbulence: Strategies for Success in Tumultuous Times." Bain & Company, Boston, 1999.

Rumelt, Richard P. "Diversification Strategy and Profitability." *Strategic Management Review,* 3 (1982).

———. "How Much Does Industry Matter?" *Strategic Management Review,* 12 (1991).

Schmalensee, Richard. "Do Markets Differ Much?" *American Economic Review,* June 1985.

"Shareholder Scoreboard." *Wall Street Journal,* 24 February 2000.

Sheff, David. "Sony's Plan for World Recreation." *Wired,* November 1999.

Silberman, Steve. "Just Say Nokia." *Wired,* September 1999.

Simison, Robert L., Fara Warner, and Gregory L. White. "Big Three Car Makers Plan Net Exchange—GM, Ford, DaimlerChrysler to Create a Single Firm to Supply Auto Parts." *Wall Street Journal,* 28 February 2000.

Simons, Fran. "Transforming Change." *Australian Financial* Review, 26 March 1999.

Sirower, Mark. "What Acquiring Minds Need to Know." *Wall Street Journal,* 22 February 1999.

Sloan, Allan. "80's Deals Showed American Express Could Use a Dose of Street Smarts." *Washington Post,* 16 March 1993.

Sohr, Steve. "Again, It's Microsoft vs. the World." *New York Times,* 13 February 2000.

"Spinning It Out at Thermo Electron," *Economist,* 12 April 1997.

Stalk, George Jr., David K. Pecaut, and Benjamin Burnett. "Breaking Compromises, Breakaway Growth." *Harvard Business Review,* September–October 1996.

Stewart, Thomas A. "Reengineering: The Hot New Managing Tool." *Fortune,* 23 August 1993.

Teece, David J., Gary Pisano, and Amy Shuen. "Dynamic Capabilities and Strategic Management." *Strategic Management Journal,* 18 (1997).

Useem, Jerry. "Internet Defense Strategy: Cannibalize Yourself." *Fortune,* 6 September 1999.

Vishwanath, Vijay, and Jonathan Mark. "Your Brand's Best Strategy." *Harvard Business Review,* May–June 1997.

Wensley, Robin. "Explaining Success: The Rule of Ten Percent and the Example of Market Share." *Business Strategy Review,* 8, no.1 (1997).

WorldScope Database provided by Disclosure First Contact. One of the most comprehensive data sources on public companies worldwide, containing financial information on more than 8,800 companies.

Wysocki, Bernard Jr. "Corporate America Confronts the Meaning of a 'Core Business.'" *Wall Street Journal,* 9 November 1999.

Yoffie, David B., and Michael A. Cusumano. "Judo Strategy: The Competitive Dynamics of Internet Time." *Harvard Business Review,* January–February 1999.

Index

About the Authors

CHRIS ZOOK is a Director of Bain & Company, a global business strategy consulting firm. He leads the company's Global Strategy Practice, is an architect of many of its Internet-related initiatives in consulting and investing, and serves as a member of the Bain Management Committee and of its Investment Committee. During his seventeen years at Bain, Zook has specialized in developing strategies for information and technology companies concerned with finding directions for new growth and building capabilities to accomplish their missions. His clients have ranged from large corporations in the computer business to small technology companies to start-up incubations in bainlab to venture funds themselves. His current focus is on developing reliable processes for finding profitable growth and building business systems to realize these opportunities. Zook has also worked outside of Bain in the private equity business.

JAMES ALLEN is CEO of eVolution Global Partners, a global venture capital firm founded by Kleiner Perkins Caufield & Byers, Bain & Company, and the Texas Pacific Group. eVolution helps corporate partners build new, independent e-commerce businesses. Allen spends most of his time working with CEOs to spin off businesses that require the capital, business-building skills, and separate equity and compensation structures necessary to compete against Internet start-ups. Previously he was a Director of Bain & Company, where he led global strategy projects with technology, consumer products, and media firms in more than twenty countries; co-led Bain's strategy practice; served on the company's board; and helped establish its private equity and venture capital practice in Europe. Prior to entering the business world, Allen worked in the U.S. government, focusing on U.S.-Soviet trade and security issues.